Teaching in UK Secondary Schools - a PGCE, School Direct and NQT Starter Guide for that Long Road Ahead
By
Hari Indran

Published 2014 by TechLearn Limited
http://www.techlearn.org.uk
Copyright © 2014 Hari Indran

ISBN-13: 978-1502552204
ISBN-10: 1502552205

The image used on the book cover is courtesy of:
https://www.flickr.com/photos/cleopold73/5677296594
The use of the image is governed by this license: https://creativecommons.org/licenses/by/2.0/

All rights reserved. No part of this publication may be stored in retrieval system, reproduced, copied, distributed, or transmitted in any form or by any means, including photocopying, recording, or other electronic or mechanical methods, without the prior written permission from TechLearn Limited. Contact details are available from http://www.techlearn.org.uk.

As per the Copyright, Designs and Patents Act, 1988, Hari Indran is identified as the Author of this publication, through TechLearn Limited.
This publication does not contain all information on the subject of secondary teaching. It is suggested that further publications are engaged with to gain a more complete picture. This publication not designed to meet the specific individual needs of any teacher, trainee, school or institution.

Hari Indran and TechLearn Limited take no responsibility for any action that occurs as a result of using this publication, and accept no liability under any circumstances for any economic losses or any loss of goodwill or reputation. Furthermore, no liability is accepted for any indirect or consequential losses of any nature. No responsibility is taken for any errors and no warranty is offered against errors, omissions or misleading statements contained in the publication. You will grant Hari Indran and TechLearn Limited absolution from and against all claims, actions, demands, proceedings, damages, costs, charges and expenses arising from your use of this book. By reading this publication, you agree to these terms.

All characters appearing in this publication are fictitious. Any resemblance to real persons, living or dead, is purely coincidental.

Table of Contents

Dedication 4
1. The journey begins... 6
2. Entry into teaching 8
3. Organisation 13
4. Your classroom 26
5. Planning lessons 28
6. Workload, responsibilities and hours 32
7. Health and stress 39
8. Working with Colleagues 45
9. Parents evenings 47
10. Technology 50
11. Technology - part two 55
12. Promotion and jobs 58
13. Managing your students 61
14. The Government and ever changing policy 63
15. The stats matter! 65
16. Rewards used to motivate your classes 67
17. Going beyond the academic curriculum 70
18. Form tutor expectations 72
19. The school engine 76
20. Unions, strikes, pay and retirement 79
21. That theory is useful! 81
22. Be yourself (*or my excuse for a story*) 82
23. Reflection 86
24. Give it time 88
25. Life after teaching 90
26. Wider challenges 91
27. Twitter heaven 98
28. A summary 105
29. The end 106
30. Coming soon to a Kindle near you 108

Dedication

I dedicate this book to the following stakeholders:

1) Any student I have taught over the last decade.

2) Any class I have observed.

3) Any form group I have had the pleasure of guiding.

4) Any teacher I have had the pleasure of working with.

5) Any school I have been fortunate enough to work in.

6) Any parent I have ever been in contact with.

7) Any university or school staff that played any part in my training during my PGCE year.

8) Any IT technician that has fixed computer equipment for me.

9) Any other technician that has ever prepared anything for me.

10) Any administrative staff that have sent letters and postcards out on my behalf.

11) Any reprographics staff that have put up with my immense photocopying requests.

12) Any receptionist that has fielded phones calls for me.

13) Any exams officer that has put up with my incessant queries.

14) Any grounds staff that have put up with my late working hours.

15) Any head of department that kept me company during long meetings.

16) Any head of year I have worked under.

17) Any school or department that I have had the pleasure of visiting whilst working within Initial Teacher Education.

18) Any exam board I have marked for.

19) Any moderator that has moderated my students' work.

20) Any external agency I have communicated with.

21) I would even like to thank the Labour (1997 - 2010) and Conservative Governments (2010 - ?).

You have ALL helped to influence my life as a teacher through experience. These experiences have led me to where I am today, and have helped me to write this book.

I would like thank my family, for their continuous support over the years. They have stood by me as I have embarked on my journey through the teaching profession. Their patience and understanding as I have worked hard, spending long hours committed to my job, has been very much appreciated. Without my family's support, guidance and love, I would have nothing.

Finally, I would like to thank my World of Warcraft MMORPG guild - a guild who kept me company whilst I would work into the late hours of the evening or early morning. Your humour, support and friendship has made the last decade special. To you, I say "moo!" Every teacher needs a hobby, and I am glad I found you!

1. The journey begins...

Ladies and gentleman, let me introduce myself. My name is Hari Indran. Why have I written this book? My career in education has started its tenth year. This book is a reflection on what has worked for me. I hope this reflection will help anyone who wishes to get into teaching at any level, but is aimed particularly at those who want to enter the Secondary sector.

If you are someone who has worked in industry and is thinking of getting into teaching, this book will provide some insight into what you can expect. If you are someone who is in their final year at university and are contemplating a life in the classroom (through the School Direct, Teach First or PGCE programmes), this book will give you a better understanding of what to expect. If you are a PGCE student who has completed your training year, and are preparing to do battle in your NQT year, this book will hopefully give you a useful checklist to apply against your teaching practice.

So what qualifies me to publish this book? Well firstly, it is a labour of love. It is something I have always wanted to do. If anything in this publication helps you to improve as a practitioner, then I will have accomplished my goal. During my career, I have worn many different hats, as a Computing and ICT teacher, ICT Co-Ordinator, school based PGCE and NQT mentor, and a university teacher trainer. This book is an amalgamation of my thoughts and strategies utilised over the last decade. My own experiences as a teacher as well as my visits to dozens of schools over the last decade help to inform my thinking.

Over the years, I have given advice to many people who have been in two minds over whether to enter teaching. I have counselled many trainees who have completed their first year of teaching, but did not fully comprehend what was coming. This book is designed to be a short read and to the point. I don't use lots of complex technical terminology. Digested hopefully within a couple of hours. A flavour of what the teaching profession has to offer, but also an insight into what steps to take in order to be successful as a new teacher. The book covers a number of different aspects, such as planning, organisation, technology and 'teaching life' in general. It doesn't cover the ins and outs of behaviour management or the pedagogy behind teaching your specific subject area. Both of these aspects are covered expertly in a variety of other books.

Feel free to pick and choose what chapters to read. Some chapters will be more useful for NQTs, Teach First and School Direct staff, as opposed to PGCE beginner teachers. Some of the chapters (two, three, five, eight, nine and twelve) provide scenarios or questions at the end, which can prove a useful discussion point with colleagues or at university.

My expectations have always been high. I have always put my heart and soul into my teaching, giving it 110% (sorry to use tired and old clichés). This book invites you to take a look into my mind, trawling through my experiences in the profession, seeing what has worked (or not worked) for me. Hopefully what has worked for me, may work for you.

If you are happy to continue, let us begin our journey. Pull the lever, close the hatch and let us fly away. Check the fuel tank first though. This profession needs energy, drive and commitment!

2. Entry into teaching

There is no point starting on a journey, unless you really are determined to travel down that long road ahead. A journey is also pointless unless you have a reason to travel. Wasted journeys are a waste of everyone's time. Your time. The school's time. The students' time. This chapter involves doing some honest soul searching. Why do you want to teach?

Don't assume entry into the teaching profession is smooth. It isn't. There is a stigma associated with teaching in the UK. Based on my conversations with the general public in steam rooms, MMORPG chat rooms, trains, shops, pubs and family gatherings (yes, such a diverse sample), it would appear that some are happy to put teachers down as 9am to 3pm part-timers. Then I pose the question, "Would you ever consider being a teacher?" They laugh it off, and say that they wouldn't have the patience needed to deal with difficult students.

The entire argument presented above (from both ends) is of course flawed. It is emotive, based on one's love of doing their job. A need to defend your profession when others provide criticism. Teachers work hard. People who do other jobs work hard too. What I am trying to say, is don't be swayed by any stigma that says teaching is easy. That stigma may be derived from friends, family, colleagues or the media. Wherever it comes from, teaching is worthy of your time and commitment. It is a special profession. A profession that lets you directly shape the future of a nation. Very few other professions can claim that.

If you are keen to enter the profession, undertake a skills and personality assessment. List out your strengths. List out what needs improvement. Think rationally and carefully, and also ponder the following points:

1) Should I enter the teaching profession?

2) Do I really want to enter the teaching profession?

3) Why do I really want to enter the teaching profession?

4) What makes me qualified to really want to enter the teaching profession?

5) What personal qualities do I have which will help me succeed in the profession?

6) Do I know EXACTLY what is involved in the teaching profession?

7) Do I know EXACTLY what is expected of me in the teaching profession?

8) Have I spoken to anyone that works in the profession?

9) Have I spent any time visiting a school, to see what things are *really* like? Not just one school, but perhaps a range of different schools.

Make sure that you honestly assess whether teaching is right for you. The last point in the list above is especially crucial. After all, teaching isn't an easy job. There are people who apply for teacher training courses without any understanding of what current-day teaching is REALLY like. Are you one of those people? Were you one of those people?

Entering a profession without a good understanding of what is involved in the daily grind is worrying. Some trainees rationalise entry into the profession, based solely on their own prior experiences of schooling as a child, going back decades. Things change. Systems change. Students and society change. Governments change. Policy changes. The demands placed on teachers change.

Some people justify their entry into the profession based on their experiences abroad, and how the style of teaching in the UK needs to marry up with those expectations. If a student misbehaves, what do you do? You call for the security guards to remove the student from the classroom! Of course. Oh dear.

Then there are people who see teaching as an easy ride. A transition from another career. Can't think of anything else to do? Well, there is always teaching! Surely anyone can do it. Isn't it 9am to 3pm? I have had fascinating conversations with people who displayed the following state of mind: *"Those students will automatically fall into line and listen to everything that I have to say for hours on end - because that is how I was educated in school decades ago. I listened to everything that my teacher said, and we spent 60 minutes copying from the board. Back then, we didn't have interactive whiteboards. No, we had blackboards. Yes, with chalk! The teacher wrote on the board. We copied. The teacher then explained it, asked us a couple of questions and then class was over. Next class."*

For many of us growing up in the 1970s, 80s or 90s, that may have been the state of play in some of our classrooms. I like to call it the 'chalk and talk' approach. Certainly, over the last two decades, things have changed significantly. One hour of chalk and talk has turned into a varied lesson with multiple activities occurring, different modes of assessment being undertaken, student-led learning, and the constant checking of progress over time. That is the reality of the modern day classroom. No doubt, it will change again. Based on what you have read so far, is being a teacher what you want to do?

On a further note, you need to be aware that your responsibilities as a teacher are significant in scope. Through being a 'teacher', you are a: stage performer, mentor, role model, motivator, psychologist, therapist, social worker, admin worker, customer services frontline agent and manager. It isn't an easy set of roles to juggle. Time is always against you.

If you are fortunate enough to have worked in another profession, use this to aid your entry into teaching. Your real life experience will give you an advantage. It will hopefully allow you to draw on real life examples to make your teaching more interesting and relevant.

My PGCE course was the hardest thing I have ever done. It was a real shock to the system. Dealing with adults is very different to dealing with children. If you are considering entry into the teaching profession, take into account not only past jobs and your own school experience, but also consider aspects that are more subtle. Consider your own daily interactions with people. Consider interactions with work colleagues, friends and family. What can you learn from those interactions? How were you perceived? What do people think of you? I strongly believe that assessing yourself using this knowledge will help support your entry into the classroom.

Do consider what type of school is right for you. There is not a one-size fits all approach. Are you after a multi-ethnic inner city state school or academy, a private school, an outer city state comprehensive, or an institution specialising in vocational education? There are so many options. Whatever you choose, one thing is certainly clear. Your reason for entry into the profession must be sound. Do you genuinely enjoy teaching? Do you understand the power that you hold? You can certainly make or break the future prospects of the students you teach.

Finally, something to ponder. What kind of teacher are you, and why are you teaching? I present to you nine classifications:

1) "I am teaching because I love the money and the pension deal is

fantastic. That six week summer break is great value! Teaching? Oh yes. I do some of that too. Sometimes."

2) "I am teaching because someone said I should do it - I think it was my school careers advisor. They said I would be good at it. So I thought I would give it a try. Why not? Nothing to lose."

3) "I am teaching because I saw those teaching adverts on television. They made it look so easy. Much easier than my previous job. Those students looked like they were truly engaged, and the teacher was in his element. Everyone was having a great time in the classroom. Everyone looked so pleased and happy to be there. I can do that easily! Sign me up now!"

4) "I am teaching because mum, dad, my aunties, uncles and grandparents were all teachers. So I am a teacher too. They did it. So I have to. Make sense?"

5) "I am teaching because I genuinely want to make a positive difference, but it is up to the students whether they make anything of it. If they succeed, great. If not, I will still be here next year, they won't be. I'll get the last laugh!"

6) "I am teaching because I know what kind of positive difference I make every day to the lives of hundreds of students. I have some direct control over their futures and destinies. Thus, I will do the best I can, in the time I am given, to aid their progression. I get a great deal of satisfaction from seeing my students succeed. I take my responsibility seriously."

7) "I am teaching because I want a challenge. I am able to work independently, make decisions by myself, and enjoy the variety of interactions that are presented to me on a daily basis. No day is ever boring, and there are new problems to solve every day. Solving these problems is what keeps me going."

8) "I am teaching because when I was at school, there was an amazing teacher who inspired me. That teacher made me realise that teaching others was my calling."

9) "I am teaching because I am passionate about my subject area, and want to impart my enthusiasm for the subject to others. I am

very good at explaining concepts, both verbally and in a written manner. Yet, I am also an excellent listener, calm in my approach, and can pick up on how others around me are reacting and feeling."

10) You are teaching because...

Where do you fit in? How many of the classifications above apply to you? As long as you are clear as to why you want to teach, and are doing it for the right reasons, we can now proceed...

3. Organisation

Ah yes, organisation. It doesn't matter how much you know. You could be a world renowned physicist who discovered the theory behind the atom. You could be the most charismatic and passionate showman in your school. It doesn't matter. If you are not organised, you will fail. Simple. Or, you will keep swimming, but will start to sink. The sinking process is a slow one. Then there comes a point where it accelerates so sharply, that you can't reach the surface again. Usually, this happens in May or June for the disorganised teacher, when they realise they haven't covered enough of the exam specification before the upcoming exam!

One of my biggest strengths over the years has always been my ability to be organised, and to help others be organised. If you are thinking of entering the profession, let me give you a small taste of what I think it takes to be organised. Yes, I place high demands on myself. Some people would look at the contents of this chapter in totality and view it as rather over-the-top. Still, better to be prepared. Better safe than sorry.

The immediate essentials

The items in this list are essential as far as maintaining your organisation and sanity. You may say that your task list is committed to memory and therefore there is no need to worry. Memory? Unless that memory is photographic in nature, I would worry!

1) **School planner** - map out your daily school routine, noting class tasks for each day and activities before and after school. You can also enter key marking deadlines from your schemes of work. My preference has always been a daily planner with one A4 page representing each day. I feel constricted by A5 planners. My notes tend to be detailed, hence A5 planners never provide me with the space I need.

2) **School diary** - to map out key long-term events. It is best to note these in a diary, and not in your messy school planner, where they can get lost in all of the scribble. This can be A5. You will want to collate dates from your school calendar and any other key sources. You may wish to put important dates and events from your personal life into this diary too. This mixes work and home life, however it is useful for avoiding conflicts.

3) **The daily task list** - you go from a school diary (long-term), school planner (medium and short-term), to having a daily task list (ultra short-term). The task list supplements the school planner and is used for pressing daily issues - often when you have run out of room in your school planner, or can't make sense of the scribble. The daily task list is forever in your hand, always in front of you, even when you are actively teaching. It is a constant reminder of what needs doing **now**. Perhaps it is on paper, or if you want to be fancy, on your phone or tablet. For some of you, a separate daily task list won't be required. The use of your school planner will be sufficient.

4) **The sub task list** - for those crazy days when the daily task list isn't enough. Made on a scrap piece of paper and thrown away immediately once crossed out.

5) **The sub sub task list** - you could consider using... no... let's not go there.

You really want to try and get your planner and diary sorted before the start of the September term. Ideally, you also want all important deadlines for the first half-term (or term) entered into your planner and diary before your first day of teaching. This allows you to think ahead and anticipate key events.

Managing tasks

So you have your diary, planner and daily task list. Now what? Well you need to learn how to manage your tasks. Surely, it is as simple as crossing off tasks? No. Not really. Well, that is one element. Crossing off completed tasks is very therapeutic. However, there is one other element which is more crucial: changing the order of tasks. Teaching is a busy job. When new areas of responsibility get thrown in your direction, you will struggle to balance your usual teaching load with these extra duties. So prioritisation becomes critical. This involves moving items up and down your task list, or numbering by priority. Master this, and you will be fine.

A hot topic of debate with colleagues has often been whether one should go paperless or stick with paper? Storing task lists electronically has advantages. Electronic lists can be backed up. Losing paper is all too common. However, for those of us who grew up in the 'paper generation', having a paper task list in front of you feels right for some reason. There is something comforting about it. My solution to losing paper is simple. Keep all of the most important bits of paper together in one folder. You carry that folder everywhere you go. Yes everywhere. Long-term plans and task lists can be kept electronically and translated down onto paper as needed. So we have ended up with what I call 'blended task lists' - no relation to 'blended learning'. Yes, my teaching jokes are bad.

Your mark book

One key area to consider is how you will track class progress. The traditional method of tracking is the teacher's mark book - containing lots of grids, squares, symbols, ticks and crosses. Over time, some teachers have evolved this process to consider the use of tracking spreadsheets, allowing for automation and easier editing of your data. You can also colour your data in using conditional formatting (lots of fun) - green means good progress, red means not so good progress. If you want to be brave, you can even introduce a third colour! Most go for yellow (traffic lights).

Whatever system you use to track progress, there are two things that should be considered first and foremost. Firstly, utilising a coherent coding system is critical. Spend time designing your system in advance. What does a tick mean? What does a cross mean? What does a star mean? What does a squiggly line mean? What does a smiley face mean? What does ++ mean, compared to +++? Develop your system and stick with it. Secondly, ensure there is space for contextualised commentary. This is crucial to help jog your memory later, i.e. during parents evenings.

Quoting from this data bank makes you truly sound like an expert: "Joe Bloggs completed an excellent research task on computer hardware on 05/07/2014, and was able to show a clear link to the outside world, with excellent examples used in context. I was impressed, given that he had been absent for the previous two weeks and took the time to attend after school revision sessions. His understanding of CPU architecture was excellent - represented very clearly through diagrams, and confirmed by his test score of 88 out of 100."

The task and date are noted in the table column. 'EE' could be your code for excellent examples. The attendance at after school revision sessions could be noted as 'AS'. His test score would be noted as a percentage, perhaps translated to a grade. His thorough understanding of CPU architecture could be noted in a commentary box. It becomes very simple to build up a rich source of data very quickly. Any comments you make are then backed up with a real air of authority. You have clear evidence in your hands.

Electronic filing system

Planners and tasks lists are all good and well. However, what about your electronic filing system? You will most likely have a username and password which lets you access your own account on the school network. You will have a school e-mail account setup. For both your school network and e-mail accounts, a folder structure is critical. Teachers who save everything into their default documents folder or keep all e-mails in their inbox often struggle to find what they need when they need it. Below, I have listed out a sample folder structure that I maintain for my electronic school files. Very useful indeed!

Awards
Behaviour and rules
Brochures
Budget
Calendar school
Calendar and Scheme of work timings
Community service
CPD
Data Analysis KS3
Data Analysis KS4
Data Analysis KS5
Dept admin
Dept meetings
Displays
DSEF and DDP
Exam entries
Examiner reports
Form group
GCSE ICT
General
Cloud based apps
Induction
Mock exams
Ofsted
Open Evening
PGCE
PLC
Performance Management

    References
    Reports
    Seating plans
    SEN
    Sixth Form Tracking
    Sixth Form Cause for Concern
    Sixth Form Contact Home
    Sixth Form next year entry
    Targeting
    Task lists
    Training inset
    UCAS
    Y7 Resources
    Y8 Resources
    Y9 Resources
    Y10 Resources
    Y11 Resources
    Y12 Resources
    Y13 Resources

This electronic folder structure is a basic version of what I use. I haven't included my subfolders. Fashioning a folder structure that works for you is essential. Do it at the start of the academic year. Get yourself into the discipline of saving files into folders as you create them. At key points in the year (e.g. November, January, April and July), ensure that any loose files sitting in the root directory are dragged into the relevant folders. Come the end of the academic year, you will appreciate your efforts. If you could get into a time machine and revisit the start of the year, you would go back in time and thank yourself.

Do be aware of one issue. If you are using the Microsoft Windows environment, and you have multiple folders and then subfolders with lengthy names, followed by files with lengthy names, you may run into problems. Long file paths don't always play safe, especially when you account for the 260 character limit. If you are copying a file with a long file name from an external drive to your PC, and the location on your PC has a longer path than the file's original location, you may get an error message.

Manual filing system

So you have a working electronic filing system. Fantastic. However, you are likely to need a manual system too. You will deal with paperwork on a daily basis. As much as we want to operate in a paperless environment, that utopian vision has yet to become a complete reality. You will need a variety of folders, document wallets and filing cabinets to maintain an organised system. Consider the following:

1) A folder to store notes from students in your form group - regarding absence, school trips, etc.

2) A folder or tray for each of your classes to house resources, worksheets, lesson plans and other materials. Do ensure that each folder is clearly labelled with the correct class. This is especially important when you have class codes that all sound very similar - e.g. 12C-it1, 12C-id1, 12C-lc1, etc. The last thing you want is to deliver the wrong material to the wrong class! Perhaps consider colour coding the folders and trays to match the colour coding on your timetable?

3) A folder (or filing cabinet) to house exam papers and mark schemes, sorted in date order.

4) A folder to house training materials from inset courses or CPD events.

5) A folder for school trips. If you do organise a school trip, do be aware that there will be plenty of paperwork, with the paper trail spreading itself out over a lengthy time period. It is common for school trip planning to start well over a year before the intended trip date!

6) A folder to store performance management paperwork - meeting records, signed reviews, lesson observation material, etc.

7) A folder to store your schedules and task lists. This folder is critical, you should carry it around with you and never lose sight of it!

As with your electronic filing system, a good manual filing system will save the day when someone comes running up to you and demands paperwork instantly.

Remembering names

We have covered the basics behind organisation. Now onto something more scary. What about remembering student names? Picture this situation. You teach fifteen classes per week. Two year 7 classes, two year 8 classes and four year 9 classes (one hour each). There is a year 10 class (three hours), a full course year 11 class (three hours), and three short course year 11 classes (one hour each). Finally, you have a year 12 class (two hours) and a year 13 class (two hours). That adds up to twenty-one hours, a standard timetable. More importantly, that adds up to fifteen classes. Fifteen! On average, let us say that there are twenty-five students in each class. That totals 375 students. Thirty students in each class would give you a total of 450 students. That is a lot of names to remember.

I have worked with colleagues who can remember student names after only meeting each student once. What if you are bad at remembering names? Your saving grace will be class photos. Furthermore, a seating plan will help. At the start of the year, utilising an alphabetically ordered seating plan may help your brain process names and faces. Beyond that, keep using names in class, and soon you will remember. Students that you see for only one hour per week are going to be harder to remember, compared to students you see for three hours per week.

Backup plans (career saver)

Backups will save your career. Yes they will. Woe to the teacher who saves everything on a memory stick and nowhere else. Memory sticks, internal hard drives, external hard drives and other storage devices have a failure rate. I know from experience. Many years ago, a student once came to me with a dilemma. The metal end of their memory stick had fallen off. Their coursework was on it. It was due next week. A year's worth of work! I wasn't pleased at the time. However, I suggested that they visit the DT technician. The technician soldered the memory stick back together! It worked for thirty seconds, enough time to copy the work elsewhere.

As far as my own personal experiences, having two external hard drives fail on me in the same day is not fun. Students and teachers have often referred to me as the 'king of backups'. Why? I usually keep eight backups of my data. Why so many? I don't trust electronic storage devices. I am also rather paranoid about losing data. In addition to backing up to storage devices, there is also the 'cloud'. I don't trust the cloud either. By the cloud I am referring to online storage. Interestingly, the rough draft of this book was started 'in the cloud'. A month later, I tried to open it. An error came up. I panicked. An e-mail to the provider soon resolved the issue. However, my trust in the cloud was shaken. So I realised the best method was to keep both a cloud backup and my own physical backups. Blended backups! Surely that covers all bases?

There is another way to look at backups. So far we have focussed on keeping electronic data safe. You should also consider backup plans for when things go wrong. For example, your school server goes down and you can't load up your all singing all dancing electronic presentation. Do you have something paper based ready? Can't go wrong with paper (unless you lose the photocopies).

Consider a different scenario. Perhaps you have booked out a computer room to undertake a research task. Another teacher shows up and claims the room. There was a double booking! After arguing your case for a few minutes, you relent and head back to your classroom. As your students re-enter the room, panic is setting in. What are you going to do with them? The moral of the story is to always prepare your lessons with a contingency plan in mind.

The key messages to take away:

1) Your data is precious. If you lose it, it is all over. Protect it. Back it up (regularly).

2) Your lesson time is precious. If something goes wrong, ensure you have contingency plans in place.

3) Your sanity is precious. If something goes wrong, ensure your contingency plans are well thought out and easily accessible, and can be applied to a range of disaster scenarios.

Oh and one final thing. Having contingency plans in place for your lessons doesn't have to mean double the planning. Hopefully, disasters won't happen often. So a small bank of lessons and resources stored away in a filing cabinet will be of great value.

Careful with those e-mails!

Double check everything. No, triple check everything. Before you hit 'send' on that e-mail, look carefully at who is in the recipient list. Most e-mail programs now have a memory function, and will remember the most recent addresses you have used. Check that a student e-mail address has not been selected by mistake. Every day, we read about data breaches, such as civil servants leaving a briefcase in a taxi or train. Don't be someone who gets caught out by a data breach. The results can be embarrassing.

Part of being organised involves knowing who to share data with and who not to share data with. Sharing sensitive data with the wrong people can get you in serious trouble. For example, leaving your memory stick in your PC and walking out of the classroom, only to discover later that a student has taken it. This goes hand in hand with leaving your PC logged in and unlocked in a classroom (or office). This gives someone else access to your data and any other data accessible via shared school network drives. A real disaster scenario!

On a different note, a colleague once offered me some very useful advice. Never delete an e-mail. Archive it. You never know when that e-mail message from six months ago will come in handy.

Inset overload

So, you have your diary, planner, task list and electronic filing system. You have been organised enough to implement these BEFORE the September term starts. In the first week of term, there will usually be one or more inset days. If you are new to a school, lots of information will be thrown at you. There will be lots of presentations and many deadlines sent your way. You will certainly suffer from information overload. Therefore, utilising coping strategies is important:

1) Strategy one: close your eyes, bury your head in the sand and hope it all goes away.

2) Strategy two: listen intently without falling asleep, and jot notes down on a scrap piece of paper. You proceed to lose that important piece of paper within the numerous presentation handouts thrown at you.

3) Strategy three: bring your planner and diary along. As soon as a key deadline or important event is mentioned, write it down straightaway. Maintain a task list of anything that needs immediate attention over the next two days.

You probably want to opt for strategy three!

You're rich! You have inherited a class!

The title makes it sound like you have won the jackpot. No, you haven't inherited a fortune. You've potentially inherited more work. When starting in a new school, you may inherit classes that have been taught by a different teacher the year before. If everything is in place, it should be a smooth transition. If not, be prepared for some stress.

You should ask for a class handover document (if it exists). If it doesn't exist, you should set about gathering as much data as you can. This is particularly crucial if you are dealing with a year 11 or year 13 class. Start by making a 'to do' list related to the class. Set up an electronic folder to store relevant data. Look into gathering data on:

1) Prior attainment (e.g. coursework progress or prior test marks).

2) Where is class work stored or kept? You may receive a list of coursework grades from last year, but where is the work stored? Is it stored electronically, or on paper in folders? This is important, especially if the course is linear, and all coursework gets moderated at the end of the course!

3) What topics have been covered the year before - was everything from the specification or scheme of work covered as needed, or was anything missed out?

4) Which students should not be seated next to each other? What conflicts exist in the class? Which students work well together? Any interesting facts about the students?

5) What style of teaching was used last year? Did the previous teacher use any particular routines that were good for motivating the class?

Gathering this data may be a challenge, especially if the teacher who taught the class last year has left the school. You may find that the students give you more information than your colleagues!

Teaching a new course? - know your specification inside out!

Before you start teaching a course, it is vital you know what the exam board requirements are. Look carefully at the specification. It is helpful to make your own plan or scheme of work using the key headings from the specification. Trying to understand what exactly you have to teach is not always easy. Specifications can be brief, vague or poorly worded. If the content in the specification is new to you, this makes delivery all the more difficult. If you are struggling to interpret what the specification requires, there is a good chance that other teachers are struggling too.

Look for supporting textbooks or online materials. Although, do be careful. These materials are not always relevant, and can do more to confuse your students! Make sure that you thoroughly inspect any materials before utilising them. Also be aware that throwing a textbook at your students and relying on this as your sole teaching material is a poor move.

To understand what the specification really requires, you should take the time to look at:

1) Past exam papers - don't look just at last year's paper, go back as far as you can to get a thorough understanding of the style of questioning. Try and ascertain any patterns as far as questioning style or the frequency of topics appearing.

2) Mark schemes - examining mark schemes is absolutely critical, in that it allows you to get into the examiner's head. What standard of response is expected from students, and to what level of depth?

3) Sample coursework projects with mark allocations - look carefully at why the exam board has allocated certain marks for key sections, and read the justifications very carefully. Look to see what has changed year to year.

4) Examiner reports - this is perhaps the most useful (but underused) tool at a teacher's disposal. The report will provide you with a serious insight into what the exam board are looking for, as far as good practice and practice to avoid.

5) Teacher notes - some exam boards (e.g. AQA) may publish teacher notes documents, which go into incredible depth on what is expected for coursework projects.

6) Analysis of past marks - some exam boards may provide you with a secure online service, which allows you to analyse marks achieved by candidates who sat previous papers. You may even be

able to look at marks achieved for individual questions. This kind of analysis is incredibly powerful. For a year 12 student entering year 13, you can look back at their year 12 exam performance and highlight areas of exam technique that need improvement. Furthermore, if students have scored poorly on a particular type of question year after year, it perhaps informs you of areas that you need to develop within your teaching.

7) Analysis of student scripts - getting copies of scripts from previous years is incredibly helpful. Let's say you have three candidates, who achieved an A grade, C grade and E grade. Requesting the three scripts allows you to compare student writing style and to highlight what examiners were willing to accept as appropriate answers. More critically, it allows you see where ambiguity was evident in the marking process. This allows you to brief future candidates effectively on exam technique.

Your exam board is likely to have a secure website (login details can usually be obtained from your school exams officer). The secure website will give you access to the latest past papers, mark schemes and examiner reports.

Do be careful to check your exam board website for updates or changes to your specification. I had always assumed that exam boards would contact schools directly if a specification was changed. That doesn't always seem to be the case. Or rather, contact is made and the information doesn't feed down to you.

Try where possible to attend an official training course run by the exam board. Exam boards are now moving these courses online. That certainly has benefits, as far as reducing the need for travel. However, you do miss out on a free lunch!

Look into the possibility of networking with other schools, especially schools that have undertaken the same qualification for years and found success. You will not only get advice on what content to deliver, but key strategies on how to deliver the content to best engage learners.

Do be aware of certain pitfalls. Mark scheme answers can contradict answers from previous years. Standards of marking and moderation can vary dramatically. This is perhaps an unfortunate consequence of some exam boards providing such a wide variety of qualifications, and not being able to successfully quality assure the marking process or the people that are employed to undertake marking.

The scale of errors can be quite shocking. However, it doesn't appear that this will be fully addressed anytime soon.

Furthermore, there is always Government meddling to put up with. You may have read about the English GCSE fiasco from 2012. Incidents of this nature do not instil confidence in the system. Regardless, you have to work with what you are given. Do the best you can, working alongside the system. Such is the life of a teacher.

Concluding message

Remember my key message from earlier. If you are not organised, you are more likely to fail. Simple. Either that, or you will rely on others to help organise you. Ask yourself these very simple questions:

1) Can I keep a diary and/or list of events and tasks?

2) Can I monitor this diary and/or list carefully?

3) Do I promise to look at the diary and/or list at least once each day?

4) Do I promise not to lose the diary and/or list?

5) Do I know how to prioritise between tasks?

6) Can I organise my materials efficiently in both electronic and manual folders?

Also remember to consider backup and contingency plans, how to deal with new classes you have inherited, and preparation to deliver new courses you are not familiar with.

4. Your classroom

The previous chapter focussed primarily on organisation in relation to data - task lists, mark books, filing systems, backups, e-mails and class data. Let's shift our focus. Being organised also means looking after your physical classroom. There are a few important aspects that need to be considered. When inheriting a classroom at the start of the year, are there enough tables and chairs? You will hopefully receive details of your class sizes before the September term starts. Are any classes not going to fit? Who do you need to contact in order to get more furniture?

You don't want to be in a situation come lesson one, where you realise that you can't continue teaching because there are thirty students, but only twenty chairs. Are your chairs and tables of the correct height, such that students can comfortably place their hands on the desks? Effective classroom design doesn't always receive the thought it deserves when classrooms are built.

Look around your classroom. What do students see around them? Sit down in each chair. What can you see? Engaging wall displays or empty wall space? See what you can do to improve the environment of your classroom.

Most classrooms will have a teacher PC - which allows the teacher to take an electronic register, or control materials to be viewed via an interactive whiteboard. What direction are you facing when you sit at the PC. Is your back to the class? That is a potential recipe for disaster (depending on the class)! A small amount of remodelling can make all the difference.

Furthermore, if you sit at the back of your classroom, how easy is it to see the whiteboard? If you use presentations frequently, is the text large enough? If you are using other software, does it allow you to zoom in? Do you know how to zoom in?

When your students enter the classroom, what can they see? Do they see you at the door, ready to greet them as they enter? The act of greeting your students at the door can allow you to ascertain any problems right from the very start, and deal with them immediately before entry into the classroom. For example, a student may approach looking upset, having had a bad experience in a previous lesson. Alternatively, a student may approach in a noisy or boisterous manner. You now have the opportunity to calm them down immediately, before the lesson starts, without drawing attention to the situation.

When your students enter the classroom, what can they hear? I have worked with teachers who like to play calming music. Perhaps you want to experiment with playing different types of music.

You really want to make your classroom your own. When students enter, what can they see, feel, hear (or smell?) that makes your classroom standout?

5. Planning lessons

If you are training to be a teacher, expect to run through all of the usual planning procedures. Each lesson will need objectives, measurable outcomes and differentiation. You will need to specify how you will measure progress over time. Doing this for every lesson on your timetable can be quite time consuming and certainly stressful. Although, it does give you a good grounding in planning etiquette. A class context sheet becomes useful too, noting key information about groups of students.

Soon, you will come to realise that some experienced teachers teach without a 'full' lesson plan. A set of bullet points in their planner is their guide. Yet resources are fully differentiated, work marked on a regular basis, and progress effectively (and efficiently) monitored over time! Adapting your planning philosophy whilst moving from PGCE to NQT to experienced teacher can feel strange. However, regardless of your level of experience, planning is always required.

If your lesson is not planned, students can see through you very quickly. Lessons descend into chaos and order collapses. I have always respected Modern Foreign Languages teachers, who have to ensure each lesson is filled with a series of short and sharp activities. Activities are completed swiftly one after another in order to maintain student engagement. Not an easy thing to do for twenty-one hours per week! I recall observing a French lesson during my PGCE year. The end of that one hour was exhausting for me as a mere observer. Yet the students were engaged, focussed and learning. However, I do know that the amount of time spent planning that one lesson was immense. It was a real eye-opener for me, as far as truly understanding the realities of teaching.

If you are a PGCE, School Direct or Teach First entrant, ensure you have the opportunity to observe teachers of other subjects. If you are undertaking your NQT year, it is worth doing some further observations, since you will always pick up little techniques, hints or tips, which will potentially save you at some point during one of your own lessons.

I referred earlier to the changing times. 'Chalk and talk' lessons have been replaced with interactive, engaging, student-led lessons, filled with a variety of activities, moving at a good pace, with learning checked constantly, with progress over time evident, and getting a round of applause at the end. Alright, I exaggerate a little. The round of applause is optional. Regardless, the current teaching of lessons in schools is probably different to when you were in school. You need to be prepared to put the time into planning lessons which fit with your school's ethos, culture and way of doing things. Every school is different.

You also need to plan lessons which will get the Ofsted seal of approval. Most importantly, your lesson planning must ensure that your students can engage successfully and make progress over time. Put simply, they need to be able to learn and demonstrate that learning. Now that may sound silly. Surely, that is what teaching is all about? Yet, I have seen lessons over the years where no learning actually occurs. It is worth asking yourself a question. In my subject area, in my school, how is it that I can engage my students to learn successfully? Class 8C on a Friday Period 5 is different to Class 8F on a Monday Period 1. Every class is different. Every class has its own unique needs, and therefore requires its own specific planning. Depending on how many classes you teach, that can add up to a lot of planning.

Nobody said planning was an easy process. It's not just about planning resources for lessons. Thinking. Strategising. Putting those strategies into place. Monitoring to see if they work. Adapting those strategies. Seeking advice from other teachers. The planning process continues. It never ends. Plans need to be revised. Strategies changed. Are you prepared for all eventualities?

Picture this scenario. It has been a tough day with 7D. You are trying to work out the best way to engage two members of the class. You think it over during dinner, and then send an e-mail to a colleague asking for advice. No luck. You prepare for bed. Your routine usually involves watching two episodes of your favourite television show before falling asleep. You are just about to fall asleep, and then suddenly, it hits you! EUREKA! You have figured it out! You go straight to your notepad and pen at the bedside table. You scribble down some notes. The following day, you execute those notes, putting your plan into action. It worked. Both students from 7D were engaged. Everything worked out. The moral of that story? Inspiration comes to you during the strangest of times. When it does come, be prepared to write it down! Otherwise you will have forgotten by the following morning.

Look at the other scenarios below. How would you fare?

Scenario A. It is November. You have had the year 9 class for two months. You have understood the class dynamics and needs. You have figured out that Charlie should not sit next to John. You understand that Sarah works best when seated next to Fred. You know that Jack needs differentiated materials with key words underlined and translated. Your seating plan is in place. You have an excellent relationship with the class and your lessons have been rated good and then outstanding. It is a cold November morning, you are busy conducting a question and answer session. There is a knock at the door. The door opens and a student enters your room. He looks nervous and mentions that he is new to the school. You place the student in a spare seat. The lesson continues, and despite laying down your expectations, you start to see low level disruption occurring. The new student doesn't get along well with others. You learn later that he had moved to the area from another school, has already engaged in confrontations with several other students, and has severe learning difficulties. What do you do? Are you able to adapt your planning accordingly? In some schools, new students entering your classroom without prior warning is an all too common reality.

Scenario B. It is a warm Spring morning. Time for a department meeting. Someone remembered to bring the cookies this time! Fantastic you think. Then your head of department drops a bombshell. Your syllabus is changing. Part way through the year. Instead of entering the students for exam board A, you will be utilising exam board B instead. The reason? Exam board A has a history of poor results and issues with marking. The senior leadership are not keen on risking this year's results. You have the weekend to get your head round the new specification. Thankfully 80% of the theoretical content matches between the two boards, however, the administrative procedures are slightly different. Furthermore, a new coursework task will have to be undertaken. The previous task is now obsolete. Taking this into consideration, what is going through your head? Are you able to adapt your planning accordingly? Are you prepared to put in a huge amount of extra time over the next two months to ensure your students get through?

Scenario C. You teach History, working alongside a department of six. Except at this department meeting, only five of you are present. Your head of department indicates that one member of staff has become seriously ill, and is not likely to be back for five months. The school has opted to bring in long-term supply staff to cover your colleague's lessons. Your responsibility is to work with the supply staff, to ensure that resources are provided. Marking will be spread out between the five members of the department. You are not sure if one supply teacher will cover the entire five month period, or if you will be dealing with multiple staff. Your initial reaction may lean towards panic. After that, are you able to adapt your planning accordingly? Do you know what courses your colleague was teaching? Are you able to pick up the ball instantly and run with it?

Scenario D. It is the first week back in September. You are teaching an A Level course. It is clear however that John is not suited for the course. Not only were the entry requirements just barely met, but John really doesn't want to be there. He doesn't see the point, and to quote

John: "This work is looooong." How can you motivate John? Furthermore, how do you plan for him in your lesson plans and differentiation?

The four scenarios reflect very real situations in schools. It is natural to feel somewhat stressed to begin with. It is also worth noting that scenarios B and C are rare in most schools. However, these situations can always be resolved. It just requires appropriate planning, patience, persistence, and sometimes a bit of luck combined with a small miracle.

6. Workload, responsibilities and hours

"So, teachers don't work hard."
I say... "what?"
"Oh, teachers only work 6 hours per day and have those long holidays."
I'll say it again. "What?"
Exactly. My reaction when some people have endeavoured to discuss teacher working hours with me.

Before we consider working hours, look at these lists. I have tried to account for *some* of the various typical responsibilities that a classroom teacher would need to consider, followed by *some* of the additional responsibilities undertaken by a head of department.

Classroom teacher responsibilities

Classroom teacher responsibilities may include the following:

1) Plan your lessons - differentiating for all ability levels.

2) Plan your resources - for each lesson, for a variety of courses, allowing for differentiation.

3) Write reports and feed the system with assessment data - termly, weekly, daily?

4) Maintain updated classroom displays.

5) Progress tracking and analysis for each class.

6) Contact home to parents (writing just one letter or making one phone call is more time consuming than you think).

7) Mark work for each class (could be on a weekly basis) - you could have anything from five to fifteen classes per week.

8) Attend parents evenings, host open evenings and induction days.

9) Undertake pre-school, break and lunch duties.

10) Offer after school support for your classes - i.e. 'catch-up sessions'.

11) Many schools go beyond the 9am to 3pm day now - extended lessons after school, before school, on Saturday's and during holidays!

12) Maintain classroom behaviour to a standard which allows for outstanding teaching - much easier said than done.

13) Attend staff training events - or as is more the norm now, you are the trainer who carries out the training.

14) Cover lessons for absent colleagues (it could be for any subject).

15) Contribute to whole-school events (e.g. extra-curricular clubs that are not subject related).

16) You are likely to be a form tutor as well - you will check uniform standards, monitor student attendance and punctuality, contact home to check on student attendance, hold meetings with parents, teach your tutees how to be good citizens (PSHCEE), be there to listen to your tutees' problems and follow them up (social, emotional, behavioural problems), track the academic progress of your tutees, place your tutees on progress reports... oh I better stop there.

17) Most importantly - you must be a positive role model for your students, maintaining a strong presence in the classroom, displaying exemplary behaviour, whilst also being a good listener and reader of minds, alongside earning the respect of your students. A sense of humour also helps. Easy, right?

Head of department responsibilities

The exciting life of a head of department. You need to be a leader, someone who can be trusted to take charge of difficult situations and provide solutions. Beyond this, there is all of the below - a lot of it is administrative:

1) Monitor and track daily and weekly progress of department staff - in terms of course delivery, maintaining standards in lessons, etc.

2) Data analysis of student grade outcomes by course and by year group - utilising half-termly assessment data.

3) Overseeing interventions for groups of students.

4) Contact parents and undertake meetings (intervention after teacher strategies have not succeeded).

5) Department self evaluation documents to be completed, monitored and tracked.

6) Performance management of department staff - utilise a range of data to monitor staff ability to meet targets, what interventions to put into place to support staff, and judgements on whether to support staff pay progression.

7) Checking reports - for structure, flow, message and grammatical errors.

8) Maintaining exam entries and procedures - this is harder than you think, especially if you run a multitude of different courses.

9) Open evening oversight - production of departmental literature and displays.

10) Mentor PGCE students and oversight of their paperwork on a weekly basis.

11) Setting departmental homework projects - which are differentiated and suitable for delivery across year groups.

12) Looking after department budget and stock - anticipating what items are needed for the future, and juggling this with immediate needs, whilst faced with constrained budgets.

13) Timetabling and rooming - again, a lot harder than you think, given the need to juggle classroom capacity with the sizes of incoming classes, yet everyone wants to be in the nicest classrooms.

14) Oversight of moderation procedures - ensuring everything is ready by the required date, with all paperwork maintained.

15) Lead department meetings - ensuring pertinent issues are discussed in the time allocated, whilst allocating actionable tasks to staff.

So, you have a flavour of *some* of the typical responsibilities undertaken by a classroom teacher. I have always felt that teaching comprises of two jobs. One job is the actual teaching and extra-curricular sessions (i.e. what gets done during the day face-to-face with the students). The second job is the administrative role that goes alongside it, comprised of marking, planning, contacting parents, tracking of student progress, writing reports, etc. If you take on responsibility or additional duties (e.g. as head of department), that adds to your workload. Consider that to be a third job.

Thinking back to the earlier chapter on organisation, if you schedule tasks out carefully across the week, you can maximise your efficiency. You can plan ahead, prioritise on certain tasks, and ensure that the right amounts of time are allocated to particular tasks. A teacher who is not organised often ends up with a million tasks to do at the last minute and is unable to cope.

Now onto everyone's favourite discussion point. The actual working hours. Despite everything I have shown you so far, there will be some that still say teachers don't work hard! They are only contracted from 9am till 3pm! Teachers do work very hard, just like everyone else in the working population. I am proud to say that I have been told consistently over the years that I need to work fewer hours and that I do too much. I have always felt honoured that people respect the time and hours I put in. In my opinion, the more you put in, the more you get out of teaching.

Yet, some would argue that working long crazy hours is a sign of not working smartly enough. I would counter that with the following. Consider a teacher with a lot on their plate. Attending to multiple exam and coursework classes, whilst juggling a set of departmental and whole-school responsibilities. Let's add something further to the mix. This teacher is also a perfectionist and leaves nothing half-done. Perhaps this teacher has no choice. Working the long hours may well be deemed essential in order to get the job done properly and to the high standards expected.

However, an inability to sensibly manage your hours does take a toll on you over time. Teaching is after all a yearlong marathon. If you run too fast at the start of the race, you burn out by October half-term. I know the feeling, and it certainly isn't ideal.

So what hours should you really work? This is a question I have been asked frequently in the past by trainee teachers. Not an easy question to answer. There is no answer. Every school is different, and thus the number of hours you work will be dependent on a number of factors. Some of these factors were briefly alluded to above. Let's break them down:

1) Each school will have its own ethos. You will feel it in the air. You will see it all around you. You will feel it in your heart and in your bones. In some schools, everyone is out by 4pm. In other schools, people stay late until they are completely satisfied.

2) The number of courses you teach will have a significant impact on your hours. Take for example, a member of staff with one exam group on their timetable. Compare that to a staff member with seven exam groups to cater for.

3) Linked to the above point, is the amount of A Level teaching you have. A large A Level timetable can be incredibly time consuming to plan and mark for, given the level of depth required at key stage five. On top of that, you may have A Level classes which are large in size (over twenty students for example). That can add significantly to your marking load.

4) The propensity for change in your subject area also plays a big role in your working hours. Your subject may stand still with few changes over time - your core syllabus pretty much remains the same. Alternatively, your subject could be in constant flux, with changes every couple of years - either in terms of needing to deliver new courses, existing courses being adapted or Government initiatives to change the curriculum. You can soon find yourself in an endless planning and re-planning loop.

5) If you take on additional responsibilities, be prepared to work for the extra pay! Balancing your additional responsibilities alongside your standard teaching workload can become a real challenge. You may find yourself dependent on other members of your department to support you, whilst making the transition.

6) Finally, working hours can be dependent on one very small but

important detail. When the timetables for next year are constructed, are you teaching the same year groups and courses as last year? Furthermore, are you teaching the same courses to more than one class within a year group (e.g. teaching GCSE History to three year 10 classes)? If the answer to both questions is yes, then you have potentially hit the planning jackpot. If you are teaching the same courses as last year, you can reuse but perfect your materials. If you are teaching one course to several classes, you can utilise the same base materials for each class, and then adapt according to their individual needs. Regardless, your time spent planning is reduced.

I said earlier that there was no definitive answer to the question of how many hours you should work. However, after accounting for the factors above, we can make a sensible guess. 8am till 3pm teaching your classes. 3pm to 4pm on extra-curricular activities. 4pm to 6pm to complete your admin tasks. So in totality, 8am till 6pm. Not bad. I call those balanced working hours. Oh, and try and rest at weekends, you need to recover your energy. Of course, at certain key points, you will meet stress bottle necks, where you will need to put in extra hours during your evenings and weekends. Moderation deadlines and exam periods are the usual culprits here.

So what about holiday time? Most teachers I know spend some of their holiday time working. Some spend more of that time working than others. Next term's lessons won't plan themselves. Those coursework projects won't mark themselves. Worst case scenario? In a one week half-term holiday, you could spend two or three days working. In a two week Easter break, perhaps it is three to five days. In a six week Summer break, perhaps two weeks? Again, it all comes down to those six factors mentioned earlier, and the extent to which they impact your teaching life.

My colleagues and friends reading this will certainly laugh at me. How can I give you advice they will say, when I would frequently work a fifteen hour day, and work through most of my holidays and weekends. My argument there is simple. It was my choice. Nobody asked me to work those hours. Teaching is a true vocation. The more you put in, the more you get out. I strongly believe that. However, your own mental and physical sanity does need to be considered. Alongside managing your working hours, you will want to manage your time outside of the profession, e.g. allocating enough time to spend with family and friends. Balance is important.

Teaching is the kind of profession which will draw you in and keep you occupied, to the point where you are doing nothing but work related tasks. After all, nothing is ever perfect. There is always something to do.

For the dedicated teacher, this can impede your family life, or your social life. As you have probably gathered, I am a workaholic, and I am happy to admit that. So managing my family and social life alongside teaching has always been a challenge.

Ah yes, the social life. 'Down time' or 'me time' is essential. More on that in the next chapter.

7. Health and stress

You get asked a question by a concerned colleague: "So, how are you today?"

You answer is not convincing: "I'm ok."

Your colleague thankfully is not convinced: "No, you look really tired. Are you sleeping well?"

You go on the defensive: "No really, I'm ok. I just had a really late night."

Your colleague is starting to see through your facade: "What were you doing all night?"

You give it up: "Well, that new scheme of work for next week needed planning. Three classes needed their work marked. I'm giving a presentation to all staff tomorrow, so had to ensure that the presentation was perfect. My laptop broke down during my planning, so I spent several hours trying to recover my files."

The stress and strain is starting to show. Your high stress levels and overly tired state lead to poor performance in the classroom. The students notice, asking if you are ok. Your colleague has spoken to the head of department and organised a meeting, in the hopes of lessening your workload. Your colleague also offers to take on some of the planning burden.

In the previous chapter, I discussed workload and responsibilities. Parallel to this, you need to have something in place to manage your stress levels. Physical and mental health both need to be considered. Both interconnect. Both impact on one-another. Positive physical health can influence positive mental health, and vice versa.

In simple terms, all work and no play makes for a very dull existence!

Physical health

In regards to your physical health, firstly consider your voice. It is your most important and valuable asset. If you can't speak, you can't teach. It is not uncommon for some teachers to develop throat or voice related problems over time, due to not looking after their health. The best piece of advice I can give you is drink water. Stay hydrated during the day. Also, try not to shout. Or rather try not to shout too much. It really isn't good for your voice. Then there is the usual advice that the Government will give you. Eat your five a day, and take plenty of exercise. My translation of that is, be sensible during the working week, then visit your favourite supermarket on a Friday evening and treat yourself to a weekend of chocolate. Ok, I am not a doctor! Scrap that last sentence about chocolate. I don't want anyone complaining to me about ill health as a result of following my advice!!

In all seriousness though, you need to eat food that will keep you sustained. What you don't want is a situation where you miss breakfast, ignore lunch and rush dinner. The result is obvious. By the end of the day, you feel absolutely shattered and drained. You can feel it in your bones! You know your body best. Perhaps some of you can get away with missing one out of those three meals.

Consider the following condition: 'wobbly legs'. Usually this is the result of rushing through lunch and not eating enough to keep you sustained till the end of the day. As my teaching career progressed, I became much better at managing my lunch. Sounds silly doesn't it. Managing your lunch. Read it again and try not to laugh. But yes, lunch does need to be managed. In the same way that you need to manage your water intake. Drinking enough water is crucial to maintaining your long-term health.

Two colleagues have recently motivated me to consider my physical fitness and health. Their daily gym workouts have inspired me to try and run at least every other night, or every three nights. Ok, sometimes, it is every four nights. Fine, you got me. Sometimes it is just speed walking on my treadmill. Still, they tell me that some exercise is better than no exercise. Their advice on burning calories has been most useful! It's like having access to a personal trainer all hours of the day, based on our frequent WhatsApp conversations. Certainly in the past, the idea of me doing exercise was laughable. A rare occurrence. Well that has all changed. I feel better for it. My colleagues have made me consider the idea of pushing myself a little further every time I exercise. This can involve running a slightly longer distance. Increasing the pace slightly. Raising the incline by a fraction. My colleagues are part of what I call my inspiration equation. Positive thinking. Positive progress.

Mental health

Now let's approach your mental health. Stress is common in teaching. Teachers are under a lot of pressure. Pressure to teach outstanding lessons whilst following forever changing Government regulations. Pressure to help students achieve excellent results. This can take a toll on you, especially if you are in a school where whole-school challenges make it difficult to accomplish this.

So what are these whole-school challenges? These are challenges that are difficult for you to influence or completely control. It could be a lack of funding leading to poor facilities. Alternatively, it could be a poor working culture in the school, where students are generally not motivated. Hence you have to work twice as hard to keep them engaged. Alternatively, it could be a lack of support from colleagues, parents or school leadership. Linked to this, is the idea of 'school politics', which can take a significant mental toll on you. The best advice I have ever received during my PGCE training year was: "Don't get involved in school politics, it isn't worth it. Keep your head down."

So, it is clear that there are serious pressure points in teaching. Doing the teaching in the classroom is just the tip of the iceberg.

So how do you manage your mental stress? Easy. Set up an obsession that is different to teaching. For me, it is maintaining my DVD collection, comprising of anime, action films, horror, US television shows, and Japanese and Korean cinema. There are sadly hundreds of DVDs, still waiting to be watched. Regardless, the retail therapy is always welcome after a stressful day at work.

Food has been a tremendous help. Get through a load of marking and that earns me an evening in front of the TV with a cookie, watching the latest episode of whatever I fancy. Not just any cookie, but giant cookies! You know the ones that are baked fresh in the supermarket. Each one accounting for over 20% of your recommended daily sugar intake. In essence, this is me utilising rewards for myself, in the same way I would utilise rewards for students in my classroom. But then, I have always had the mental discipline required to get the job done, no matter what. I have always treated my teaching responsibilities seriously, putting in whatever amount of time and effort is required.

If this discipline doesn't come naturally to you, then you will need to find other ways to motivate yourself. One cookie may not be enough. A whole pack of five cookies may be the way forward! *Or perhaps not. A way forward to the hospital may end up being the most likely event!*

Oh, and contact with family and friends. Certainly, this is of great value. It will help to ground you. Sounds silly. After all, you probably talk with or meet your family and friends every day. What I am really trying to say, is don't take family and friends for granted. Teaching is stressful. Simply talking to people you can confide in is a great stress reliever. A cathartic process that keeps the soul happy. Alternatively, you may have a colleague you can talk to, or a mentor - perhaps a tutor from university. Just make sure that they are a good listener, and can offer constructive feedback.

I worked with a colleague, who I referred to as 'the man who knows everything'. Pick a topic or subject area. You can learn more from him in a casual five minute conversation, than you can from reading an entire book on the subject. Simply talking to him on a daily basis was a great therapeutic experience, relieving some of the stresses and strains of the daily grind. I will always be grateful and thankful for his support.

I maintain a close group of friends who I play MMORPG games with. They have always been very supportive in terms of providing what I call 'long distance communication therapy'. A fantastic group of people, from all walks of life, who I can easily relate to. My conversations with my MMORPG friends did not often revolve around teaching per say, but featured politics, economics, television and film, apples and cake. Yes that's correct. Apples and cake. Mr Apple, if you are out there, you know what I mean.

Of course, with people external to your workplace, your should never reveal anything specific about the workplace or the students you teach. That would be a breach of trust. Remember, you are a professional.

Exercise. We covered this earlier as far as the physical benefits. Mentally, the benefits can be more pronounced. The process of undertaking exercise can be strangely cathartic. Headphones go in, treadmill starts, and away you go. Oddly though, my preference is a sauna or steam room. The ultimate way to relax. Seriously. People find it odd I can sit in a sauna for over sixty minutes, and then walk away conscious. Seriously though, if you decide on the exercise, sauna or steam room approach, take care of yourself physically. The last thing you want is to overdo it and then call in sick the following morning. I take no responsibility if you faint in the sauna! Regular breaks are essential.

Music is another key ingredient in the relaxation recipe. Over the years, my colleagues have introduced me to new music genres. Genres I never would have considered before: classical, rap, jazz, j-pop, new age, ambient, rock, pop, electronic, R&B and world music. A colleague would play world music on a daily basis - we must have covered every country by the time he retired. My appreciation for different genres grew. It has got to the point where when someone asks me what kind of music I listen to, I simply say "everything." Finding the right kind of music to fit your mood is a worthwhile endeavour. Building different playlists to suit different occasions is the way forward. You may have one playlist for marking. One for planning, and one simply for relaxing. A decent pair of comfortable headphones is certainly worth investing in.

Finally, consider reading. No, not reading more Government policy documents, exam specifications or other work related literature. Read something you enjoy. Ever since I purchased an e-reader, in the rare moments where I have found thirty minutes to sit down and read, I have managed to forget all about any daily stresses, strains and pressures. Your mind is whisked away to another location in a world of fantasy. You could also consider meditation. Perhaps a little extreme for some of us, but great if you can grasp the full benefits offered.

Above all else, getting enough sleep is perhaps the most important consideration. There is lots of research out there on how long we should sleep for. Ignore the research. Everyone is different. For me, if I go to sleep at midnight, I tend to be fine for a 7am wakeup. I feel somewhat groggy, but by 8am, I feel ok. If I go to sleep at 1am, I wake up groggy at 7am, but still feel very tired at 10am. If I go to sleep at 2am, I have no hope for the following day. If you are a PGCE student or Teach First candidate, you may well be straight out of university. You can forget those late morning wakeups and late night parties! Get the right amount of sleep that your body needs.

I understand that some of you will have family and personal commitments that need to be juggled alongside teaching. Sadly, it won't be easy ensuring that you get the right amount of sleep and rest. However, there are some shortcuts which can help you along. Consider power naps. You get home from school, having had a tiring day. You have marking to do this evening, however, all you want to do is eat and sleep. Set your alarm, and take thirty minutes out to have a nap. It will make the world of difference. Providing you wake up when your alarm sounds, you will feel better, refreshed and ready to work again!

Ultimately, teaching is more than a job. Some consider it to be a way of life. It is a truly special vocation. You need to be dedicated, passionate and keen to make a difference. If not, then this profession isn't for you. I remain convinced that across the general working population, a large proportion of people would not be able to teach successfully. Therefore, you are truly special. Your knowledge, commitment and dedication makes you extraordinary. You hold great responsibility in your hands. With great responsibility comes great workload and potential stress. However, remember one thing. Your health is most important. Look after it. Care for it. Nurture it. For without it, you have nothing.

I would have ended the chapter here. However, there is something else that comes to mind. A critical piece of advice that is most important when managing your mental stress levels: *don't take it personally*. Leaving the stress at work is the ideal solution. I can't lie to you. You will have bad days where your dealings with students, parents, exam boards or colleagues won't go to plan. You may experience poor dealings with ALL of those stakeholders, all across one day! Don't take it to heart.

Try to compartmentalise the stress in your head. Associate it with work and not with home. Worrying about it at home where you can do nothing to address it really won't help you. Switch off at home where possible. Sleepless nights fretting about these problems won't make them any better the following day.

However, there is a small problem. If you are a teacher that cares deeply about your job, making that work-home separation may be more difficult. You care so much, that you can't help but worry at home. So what can you really do? As discussed previously, occupy your mind deeply with other things - family, television, reading, social outings, etc. Do something at home to truly escape reality, and you will walk into work the next morning, fresh and ready to tackle any problems. I have found that reading an engrossing book for leisure is the biggest help. Yet, it is very much a personal choice. Certain activities will work better for different people.

8. Working with Colleagues

Your team. The people you work with. This is what makes the school go round on a daily basis. If the team is right, everything else falls into place. I can't stress that enough. A supportive department leads everyone to great success. I have been fortunate in my teaching career to have worked with some very talented individuals who understood the need to work together as a team, so that everyone succeeds.

You must learn to play well with others. A failure to do so will lead to absolute disaster. If you don't get along with the people you work with, remember why you got into teaching. You entered the profession so that you can teach. To help the students you work with. Their success and progression is your ultimate reason for existing. In order to see them succeed, it is imperative you work well with your colleagues. Anything else is a distraction from that goal.

My ethos has always revolved around being as nice as I can be to everyone around me. By nature, I can be overly generous and giving. That is who I am. That has helped me to navigate the profession. It has won me respect from teachers and pupils. It has helped my working relationships succeed.

Ask yourself something. Can I take one for the team? Can I support and cover for my colleagues in time of need? Can I be unselfish? More importantly, can I ask for help when I need it?

Schools are busy places. Your school may have a common staff room. How many staff actually convene and have lunch together? If you are not careful, your lunch times can be taken up by a variety of tasks: looking for other staff to discuss the next scheme of work, helping students who were behind on work completion, offering guidance to students on non-work related matters (mentoring meetings, etc), setting up something elaborate for your period five lesson, or completing an administrative task that should have been done before lunch. It takes a disciplined teacher to sit down for thirty minutes, have lunch and not do any work. Besides, running around school whilst chewing on a sandwich is not good for your digestive system.

One solution is to force yourself to sit down and eat lunch. Although, your willpower could be lacking. That's fine. Force yourself to sit down with other people. Combined willpower wins. As a department, you may want to consider departmental lunches once per week. Each week, someone takes a turn providing lunch for the department. My attempt at this always revolved around buying supermarket meal deals.

Other members of staff proved to be more adventurous, and actually cooked!

Consider the following scenarios. What would you do?

Scenario A. A member of staff in your department suffers a family bereavement. They take a leave of absence for three weeks, needing to travel abroad. You are asked to monitor their classes, and offer after-school sessions to ensure the key exam groups are kept on track.

Scenario B. You are teaching alongside five other members of staff. One member of staff is not pulling their weight. You notice, because students have come to see you confidentially, and have complained that their work isn't being marked. What do you do? Do you approach that member of staff directly and hope they change their approach? How long do you wait till you approach them? What if that doesn't work? Do you approach your head of department?

Scenario C. A new member of staff has joined your department. You find that their subject knowledge is not where it needs to be. You notice that they are struggling to teach certain theoretical concepts. They approach you, requesting your assistance to help them improve their subject knowledge. You would love to help, but having just received a promotion to head of year, you are extremely busy after school. Therefore, they have requested to meet with you each Saturday morning for two hours. You are about to agree, but then realise on a Saturday morning you play football. Can a comprise be reached?

9. Parents evenings

So you spend most of your week with the students. You may as well meet the parents right? Here comes your first problem. Names. This was covered in an earlier chapter. Hundreds of students taught every week. In the class environment, you have done enough to easily recognise faces, and can actually put 99% of names to faces. Wait. This is a parents evening. They are not in the classroom, sitting in an ordered seating plan. This is ad hoc. Uncontrolled. Not organised. Well, yes, there is a schedule for the parents evening, you know roughly when each student will arrive to see you with their parents. Actually, given that you teach three classes in the year group, that is approximately ninety students. The schedule disintegrates after the third appointment, and there is a queue of parents waiting to see you. So what do you do? Well, photos will definitely help. Don't panic. Most students should still arrive roughly in the order of the schedule. This should be enough to help piece things together.

Always be polite and cordial at a parents evening. Even if you are not thinking it! Professionalism is the key. Even if some students and some parents are not professional. You are the professional. So you must act like one at all times. When difficult questions get asked. When parents feel the need to rant at you or about you. It doesn't matter. Stay professional. Stay calm. Parents want to be reassured that their children are performing well. If that is true, then fine. Otherwise, you must be truthful. There is no point telling someone what they want to hear, if reality does not match up. Oh, and remember your mouth wash or mints. Definitely a must!

One final thing. Water. Stay hydrated during a three hour marathon evening where you somehow fit in ninety appointments. Your voice will thank you for it the next morning. Oh, and take more than one bottle!

Consider the following scenarios. What would you do?

Scenario A. The father arrives, temper flaring. You realise within the first thirty seconds that he is referring to a student you don't teach. Wait, you taught this student last year. The father is unhappy about another member of staff in the department who he has just spoken to. The father thinks that the teaching standards are not up to scratch. He emphasises that he wants you to teach his son and he wants a class swap to occur.

Scenario B. After an initial pleasant discussion, both parents have emphasised that the work is too easy. Tim completes his homework in minutes. It is not challenging enough. He needs to be set more homework, and the parents would like a weekly phone call to discuss progress. You look at your mark book and realise that the homework tasks set for Tim's class are extended projects, with open-ended research questions. Tim has copied and pasted. You imply to the parents that copying and pasting (plagiarism) has occurred. The parents deny that this is the case. They say they both sit down and do the homework for Tim. No wait. They correct themselves. They do the homework with Tim.

Scenario C. You are the best teacher in the world. Always supportive. Always helpful. Always respectful of the students. Always supporting students through difficult times. The most knowledgeable teacher in the profession according to Scott's parents. Scott gets along so well with you. Every teacher should be like you. This praise continues on for another five minutes. This is followed by Scott's parents giving you a package. You open it, to reveal a very expensive watch. You are flattered, but indicate it is too much. They insist that you have it. What do you do? *Well, one thing is clear - you should report expensive gifts to your school's senior management in charge of staffing.*

Scenario D. You teach GCSE ICT. The parents think that the syllabus is not challenging enough. Tom should be learning about much more than bits, bytes and megabytes. He needs to be stretched! Those exam papers you gave him for homework were too easy. They don't stretch him. Poor Tom is sitting there shaking his head. Looking at your mark book, you notice that Tom's last score reflected a D grade. His target is a B grade.

Scenario E. Katy couldn't do her research homework. Her mother explains that they have had their broadband connection cut off so Katy was unable to access the internet. They couldn't afford the bill. You indicate that computer room facilities are available after school. No. Katy must be picked up as soon as school ends. There is a schedule to keep to, with three other siblings to pick up from different schools. The mother explains that she doesn't want Katy walking home in the dark. It isn't safe.

Scenario F. Both parents are fascinated to know more about your professional background. Precisely, they want to know where else you have taught. No, not just names of other schools. They want to know about those other schools. What degree do you have? Which university did you study your degree at? Do you have a master's degree? What were your exam results like last year? What proportion of your students achieved A*-C? Do you know what their child's precise special needs are? Can you recite ten strategies to meet those special needs?

Scenario G. Jake's father sits down looking rather unhappy. Jake is not happy either. Jake hasn't made good progress this year for you. You communicate that to his father. Jake can't look you in the eye. His father is also looking down. You find out that every report so far this evening has been negative. Jake just has no interest in being at school. His father doesn't know what to do. They have tried everything at home. Shouting at Jake at home doesn't work. He just doesn't want to do his work. He sees no value in obtaining his GCSEs. Everyone has given up.

Scenario H. Sarah's mother is not happy with how you treat Sarah. Apparently you pick on her. You explain that Sarah will never stop talking, is constantly disrupting other students who want to work, and seems to take more interest in her makeup as opposed to her studies. Ah yes, the makeup kit. How dare you confiscate it? It cost £50! You indicate that you returned it at the end of the day. No. It doesn't matter. You need to stop picking on Sarah.

I am hoping I haven't scared anyone off yet. A number of these more challenging scenarios are quite drastic and certainly rare. I have found that the majority of parents are more interested in their children succeeding and will support you all the way. The key lesson here is how you react. Do you maintain a professional and calm demeanour, or do you lose your temper and start arguing?

10. Technology

Technology. Either you love it or you hate it. Over the years, schools have placed great faith in technology - to support administrative procedures and then to support teaching and learning. I remember when I attended secondary school, and my school obtained a connection to the internet. One computer in the whole school had access, and it was located in the library. We would sit and stare at it, not quite sure what to do. Things have certainly come a long way. We have progressed from PCs and laptops, to using tablets and phones. What? Tablets and phones in the classroom? Surely not!

Don't be afraid. A new era of technology is upon us, with incredible functionality and power (if used correctly). Let's say that you are a History teacher, teaching students about Roman battle formations. What are your potential options? Option one involves you lecturing them for an entire lesson. Not a good option. Option two involves the use of a text book. We have all heard it before. Read chapter three and answer all of the questions. Option three involves the use of engaging props and stories to make history come alive. Option three sounds like a good option! Wait, someone else has borrowed the props. So there is option four.

Option four involves booking out a computer room and taking your students down for a research task. In many schools, bookable computer rooms are in rare supply. So how about option five? You stay in your classroom. Each student has access to a tablet. They complete a group research task in your lesson on Roman battle formations. Each group member shares resources with one another using a shared presentation (through Google Slides). One group member is in charge of editing and proofreading the presentation, providing feedback to other group members. You can monitor the progress made by each group, since they have shared their presentations with you. You circulate around the room, offering feedback and advice, measuring group and individual progress over time, making a note in your mark book.

Finally, each group shares their completed presentation with the rest of the class. The best bits are extracted and used to form one final presentation. Using the combined material, each student answers a series of questions to test their understanding. These questions are completed using a Google Form, which then marks the answers, and provides the students with instant feedback. The results are exported into your electronic mark book and colour coded accordingly. There you have it. Technology being used in a lesson.

I mentioned Google Apps. For those of you not familiar with Google Apps for Education, it consists of a suite of online software applications (based in the 'cloud'). You can complete word processing, spreadsheet and presentation tasks, but you can access these files anywhere, providing you have an internet connection. The flexibility and functionality offered by Google Apps is excellent, with a good number of Governments, schools and universities having taken advantage of it in recent years. Best of all, schools currently get it for free!

Consider this scenario. You are planning a scheme of work on volcanoes. You are doing this alongside your head of department. You write the scheme of work in a Google Doc and create resources for lesson one by utilising Google Slides to create a presentation. You share the scheme of work and resources with your head of department. You are both at home. The head of department logs in and starts making changes to the scheme of work. You both converse via the chat feature in Google Slides, and decide the latest change is not ideal. You revert back to an earlier version of the presentation using the 'Revision History' feature.

So, the power of Google Apps for Education - well worth considering if your school has not already invested in it. Did I mention before? It currently doesn't cost anything for schools (reference: http://www.google.co.uk/enterprise/apps/education/).

My own experiences of using Google Apps in the classroom have been incredibly positive. For example, setting up hand-in folders for student work, and then providing feedback to students using a shared Google Spreadsheet, where the students can monitor their progress and grades. It is important to remember though that using Google Apps is one solution. One solution derived from a collection of solutions. It is easy to become enamoured with technology, to the point of becoming completely dependent on it.

Let's step back for a moment. Consider historical errors, where managers and policy makers champion the idea that 'technology will save us'. Other methods should be banned or eradicated. It's not that these other methods are not effective, it's just that apparently technology is superior to all of them! Such complete and utter reliance on technology is a dangerous thing. It certainly isn't the be-all and end-all solution.

Also, consider exam revision. Why print out a past paper when students could be looking at it online? Printing twenty past papers and mark schemes is an expensive endeavour. Making students revise from their screens costs nothing! Well, many of my students have often told me that come exam time, they prefer the traditional methods of revision. A tangible folder full of revision notes, which they can see and feel. The tried and tested method, going back centuries. These same students however will also have their revision notes on their phone or tablet, and will revise whilst on the bus.

So what is the key message in all of this? It is important not to force technology onto your students as a sole solution at pivotal times, when they may prefer a different solution. I have found that technology is best used alongside other methods. A blended combination, where students can then choose which methods to accentuate as exams draw closer.

Then there is the idea of using technology for the sake of using it - linked to the 'technology will save us' concept discussed earlier. This has been a problematic area over time. The idea that technology is so wonderful, and hence huge sums of money should be spent buying into hardware and software, but without any true understanding of its purpose or value. If you are coming into teaching from a previous career, you may well have experienced this. The management hold a meeting and say, we have bought into System X. Therefore, everyone MUST use it. We are not quite sure what it does, but the salesman was very convincing. Since we bought it, you WILL use it. Any questions? Oh wait. There's no time for questions. System X already needs an upgrade. Ah, there's the salesman. Oh look, a 50% discount if we buy System Y too. Look at all of the amazing things it can do!

System X and System Y. They will save your organisation, make it more productive and efficient. There will be cost savings. You can produce twice the output. Wait, how do we use it? Is there any training? Wait, it isn't doing what we asked for! 90% of the functionality is not required. System X doesn't talk to System Y. Can we get a refund? Oh. We are locked in for ten years? Oh dear.

When engaging with technology, it is crucial that we learn lessons from the past. George Santayana said, "Those who cannot remember the past, are condemned to repeat it." Educational history is riddled with failed policies and initiatives. Technology was seen as something that would transform education, changing it beyond recognition. That vision never really came to pass in the 1990s. Education is still conducted in a classroom, with a teacher and a number of students. Students still sit handwritten examinations. The scripts are then marked by humans, to varying degrees of precision. The system hasn't really fundamentally changed.

A Computing and ICT teacher championing the ways of old? Surely not! Well, I have something further to say.

Technology does now have the chance to genuinely transform learning. Wait. Transform is a strong term. It has been used haphazardly before. The academic in me promotes a cautious approach. Let's rephrase. Technology does have the chance now to genuinely *change* teaching and learning for the better. As a tool that replaces the teacher? No. Despite what some politicians and bureaucrats may have hoped for. What we have is technology being used as a tool to support learning, or to enhance it. The Google Apps examples that I provided earlier are proof of that. I can say that it has made my administrative life easier as a teacher, and enhanced learning in my classroom. It has allowed for blended learning and flipped learning.

Ok, technology has allowed for blended and flipped learning for decades. However, I have found that students have been more willing to engage with Google Apps outside of the classroom. I have memories of System X, followed by System Y being introduced, but these systems are only of worth if students engage and use them outside of the classroom.

An example may help to illustrate my point. Twenty years ago, you may have set a homework task - next lesson, we are learning about the role of the Chief Information Officer. Read chapter ten, make notes and be prepared to discuss next lesson. Ten years ago, you may have altered the task ever so slightly - next lesson, we are learning about the role of the Chief Information Officer. Research about their role online, make and/or print notes and be prepared to discuss next lesson.

Today, using tools for online collaboration alters that task significantly. Consider this plan. You will split into groups of three. There are three key questions to answer in relation to the Chief Information Officer. Each group member will pick one question to explore, and will utilise a shared presentation to collaborate with other group members. You will need to summarise your responses to the questions in bullet point form on the slides, but in the notes section, you should provide detailed justifications. One member of the group is responsible for checking the progress of each member in relation to the deadline. A second group member is responsible for proofreading the presentation. The third member is responsible for checking the validity of sources used. You can do this from the comfort of your home, not needing to travel to an agreed location in order to meet face-to-face each evening. You can chat online whilst completing the task.

Once the deadline arrives, the teacher checks the work has been completed by each group. Each group then shares the presentation with the other groups and peer feedback is provided. Action after feedback is then undertaken, with amendments made and highlighted.

The key to success here is sharing and collaboration, with technology being used to aid that process. In this scenario, technology isn't seen as a replacement for teachers, it isn't seen as the only solution to effective learning. Instead, technology is used effectively as a supporting tool. A tool that can make education a more fun and engaging process, with genuine positive additions being made to the quality of teaching and learning.

There are issues to address. If you are a teacher who is not confident with using technology, be wary. Technology used for the sake of using it is dangerous. For example: use the Internet to research topic X, copy everything you can find and print it. The end. That is technology used in a dangerous manner. The solution here is thought and time. Technology should only be used once careful thought has been placed into its implementation. You need to invest time into planning how to use technology effectively, in much the same way you invest time into planning how to use any other resource in your lesson.

A fear of change is also something to consider. Teachers who have utilised tried and tested methods to achieve results, and are therefore afraid to consider technology. The key solution here is acceptance of technology as one tool. One of many tools. Those other tried and tested methods can still be used.

I hope this chapter has provided some insight into the power of technology, yet has thrown up enough warning signs, such that any potential dangers are thought about. Speaking of dangers, the next chapter takes us in a different direction.

References and copyright notices: Google™ is a registered trademark of Google Inc. Google Docs™, Google Slides, Google Spreadsheets and Google Forms are part of the Google Apps™ service and are registered trademarks of Google Inc. For further information: http://www.google.co.uk/enterprise/apps/education

11. Technology - part two

The previous chapter considered the use of technology to support teaching and learning, inside and outside of the classroom. This chapter considers two key problems. One problem is linked to teaching and learning, as far as our reliance on the internet to source information. The second problem is in relation to social networking and its dangers for teachers.

Relying on the internet for information

You set a piece of homework. For example, find out how the carbon life cycle works, and provide real life examples of each of the main components in action. I am not a Geography teacher. My first instinct? Go to a search engine. Second instinct, look at the results on the first page and click. Actually, I don't stop at page one. I keep clicking, to see what else is buried. Most people however don't seem to travel past page one's search results, and that includes your students. A quick copy and paste job, including the complicated diagram they find, and there you have it. Homework done in two minutes. Ready to hand in. Except, of course, for those students who tell you their printer was broken and so they couldn't print their copy and paste masterpiece.

The world wide web and all of its glorious content. A blessing and a curse. There is no easy way round this. Set your high expectations from the start. Make it clear how you want your homework done. Get students into the habit of reading sources and then constructing their own arguments and conclusions. Get them into the habit of using referencing techniques (this will help them later when they undertake their A Levels and university courses). It is a good idea to recommend a series of websites that you think students should visit for each topic. There is so much rubbish out there on the web.

Get to know how your students write. Set an extended writing task in class. Take it in, and digest it. Not for the content, but for the writing style. What is their writing style actually like when they don't have access to a computer and the internet? This is critical for assessing exam technique.

Teachers and social networking

The second problem I want to discuss with you is the danger of social networking for teachers. Many of you reading this will have social networking accounts. In the summer of 2014, I created a new Twitter account: @TechLearnUK. This is different to my personal account. It is used for the purposes of work, and is a public account, accessible and viewable by anyone.

Now contrast this with your personal social networking accounts. You must be very careful with how you present yourself. Firstly, consider the privacy settings. You do not want students being able to befriend you. Ensure that you are on lockdown. My personal accounts do not accept friend invites from strangers. If I want to befriend someone, I will seek them out. My profile picture is not a picture of me. I use pictures from television shows. It is not possible to see who my friends are either. For some of you reading this, putting your social networking account on this type of lockdown will seem incomprehensible. However, it is important. Your students will be more active on social media than you. You really need to take precautions now, if only to avoid embarrassment later.

Picture this scenario. You go on a night out. You get a friend to take photos of you. Alcohol is involved. You don't look your best. You had a stressful week. You post the pictures to your personal account. Your privacy settings are too relaxed. A student finds the pictures. Come Monday morning, you receive lots of wide eyed stares. Students are whispering. You walk past a notice board. There you are in all your glory, standing on top of the nightclub table, drinking from two different pints of alcohol, all at once. You rip down the photo. Naturally at this point your mind is going into shock. You run past another notice board, and there is another photo. A few minutes later, you are in the Head Teacher's office. It doesn't end well. You struggle to get through your classes during the day, unable to field those awkward questions from students. What can you say? It wasn't you in the photo? Your long lost twin?

That evening you go home and check your inbox. Some of your friends have messaged you, indicating that the photos has been shared online and are receiving a huge amount of attention. You have been tagged too. The photos are providing a link back to your personal account. We live in an online sharing culture. Something becomes newsworthy instantly if enough people share it. The majority of the online community will have forgotten it by tomorrow. Your students however won't forget. The long-term damage to your reputation is irreparable.

Keep in mind that with social media, it isn't just your reputation at stake. Your school's reputation is also at stake. As a test, make a dummy account. Search for yourself. See what comes up. What do you find?

Would you want one of your students seeing the photos that appear? Before entering the profession, a sacrifice is needed. You discard your previous public presence. I don't mean deleting your profile. I mean starting afresh with your privacy settings. You are after all a teacher. You hold a very powerful position of responsibility, influencing the lives of your students, who will look up to you as a role model. I maintain a very active social networking presence on a personal level - but only share activity with a small circle of friends.

It is important to be aware of the numerous social networking services that exist. Also be wary of friends taking photos of you and posting those photos to their own public social networking accounts! The best advice I can give you, is don't put yourself in a position to allow for this to happen.

Let's end this chapter with another problem. We have considered the dangers of social networking for teachers. For students, it appears to be a more significant danger. Remember the good old days when problems in schools were usually started in the playground, and then ended in the playground? Student X stole student Y's football. Student Y pushed student X. Some name calling was evident. A staff member intervenes in time, and all ends well. Fast-forward to modern day society. It would appear that so many arguments and conflicts start off on social networking and then make their way into the school environment. This becomes incredibly difficult to control and fix.

Young people don't always get it right with their use of social networking. How responsible are they? Out of the thousands of 'friends' on their ever expanding friends lists, how many are actually people they know? Are they aware that what they post online may still be accessible, even if they 'delete' it? Has anyone taught them social networking etiquette? Has anyone fully taught them about the consequences? That in itself is a whole area of study, and provides one argument for a joint ICT and Computing curriculum, as opposed to a dominant Computing curriculum. That's an argument (or a book) for another day though.

Be aware of the impact that social networking can have on your teaching life. Monitor your profiles carefully. Be aware. Be astute. Be ready to act if needed.

12. Promotion and jobs

If you are seeking employment as an NQT, make sure you consider using a wide range of job procurement options. The initial temptation is to search for jobs on the TES website. That's fine. However, there are many other options to consider. Look on school websites. Sometimes, schools will post positions on their own websites, which are no longer viewable on the TES site. Send CV and covering letters out to schools, you may catch their interest. Finally, look at council websites. Whatever you do, be very careful when it comes to filling out applications. Double check, triple check and then quadruple check your spelling, punctuation and grammar. This is critical. It is not uncommon for a poorly written application to be binned straightaway!

If you are beginning your teaching life as an NQT, your first year may seem rather daunting. That's fine. Practice makes perfect. Within a few months, you will be part of the furniture. Your confidence will grow, and you will eventually start thinking about future opportunities. Most importantly, take on as little or as much as you feel comfortable with.

There is no compulsion to seek additional responsibility. Many teachers are happy just being in the classroom, doing the best job possible. They have found a happy balance between work and home.

If you are keen for promotion, decide on your motivation. Money? Midlife crisis? Gaining experience in a different environment? Extending your current knowledge base? Trying something new? Looking for a challenge? If you are keen to do more, then seek it out. Opportunities exist everywhere, both in your current school and in other schools.

It is not uncommon for an NQT to be given a promotion or extra responsibility in their first year. Certainly by your second year, it is worth thinking about what additional responsibilities you are comfortable taking on. Decide on your journey. Will you seek pastoral or a departmental promotion? Pastoral is what I like to refer to as the 'people route'. Become an assistant head of year, followed by a head of year? Are you good with tracking academic progress of a whole year group? Can you monitor their personal wellbeing and resolve any problems that come up?

Alternatively, the departmental route could see you become a deputy head of department or be responsible for a key stage. You could then progress onward to becoming a head of department.

There are also other whole-school positions to consider. PSHCEE co-ordinator? Literacy and numeracy co-ordinator? Gifted and talented co-ordinator? And so on...

Eventually, you may become an assistant or deputy head teacher. Something to aim for? Although, this isn't for everyone. You need to think very carefully about what role is right for you. Try to put the role first, and the money second.

You can also consider the international route. An adventure perhaps?

There are pros and cons to any manner of promotion, and it is important for you to weigh those up carefully before making the jump.

Would a master's degree help you? Yes, if it is in the right area. If you know that your passion lies along the pastoral road, then consider a relevant master's degree in a pastoral discipline. It will allow you to access relevant literature, to conduct useful investigations which will hopefully aid your everyday practice. A master's degree can be undertaken part-time. However, be aware of the difficulties in juggling such a commitment, alongside your full-time teaching job.

Some teachers supplement their income through tutoring. Tutoring can be a useful addition to your CV as well as a strong financial boost. Although, do take into account that the planning required for a sixty minute one-to-one tutoring session is immense!

To aid your chances of achieving a successful promotion within school, ensure you collect relevant evidence. Evidence can be in the form of e-mails which confirm your successes on projects, screenshots of systems you have created, etc.

How long should a teacher stay in one school? Three years sounds sensible. Yes, but every school has teachers that have been there for decades! Why do they stay for so long? The location may be convenient (don't underestimate the influence of travelling time on job satisfaction). They may be comfortable with the courses they deliver. They may like the department they work with. These factors all come into play, and can influence the length of time you stay in one school.

Developing a sense of loyalty to a school is no different to any other profession. Consider this scenario. Tom Smith is a lawyer working for a firm called Fisher Stevenson. He has an excellent track record of winning cases and making money for the firm. Other law firms would pay to have him. Yet he stays loyal. This isn't loyalty driven by money alone. He has ambitions to be a senior partner, and wants to do it at Fisher Stevenson. In his mind, this firm means everything to him.

Similarly, you could develop loyalty to a particular school, wanting to see that school succeed. Taking pride when it does succeed, and your name is recognised as a key contributing factor. After all, each year is different, in that new students enter and leave. Colleagues come and go. Yet you are still there, the one constant factor driving the machine to succeed. If you see your presence in a school as a long-term project, with designs on becoming a senior leader or teacher with key responsibilities, then sticking around for a while isn't a bad thing.

A roadmap of where you are heading is useful to draw out. Consider the following:

1. Where do you plan to be in one year? Two years? Four years? Ten years? Twenty years? Most importantly, how will you get there?

2. Who do you need to speak to for advice on succeeding in your journey?

3. Are you happy in your current position, does this provide easy access to the next part of your roadmap?

4. What barriers could stop you from moving forward?

5. What measures will you take to remove those barriers?

13. Managing your students

Managing your students - in some circles, this chapter heading would be rephrased as behaviour management. If you want to read about behaviour management techniques, there are plenty of books out there dedicated to listing one technique after another. I want to consider something else. Developing positive relationships with students is more what this chapter is about.

How do you want to be viewed by your students? This isn't about being liked. This isn't about being feared. Now keep in mind this is only my opinion, based on my experiences. In my opinion, being respected is what will help you manage your classes successfully.

The term 'respect'. What does it mean? Perhaps at one point in time, an assumption existed that young people would give their elders respect automatically. Or is that compliance, rather than respect? Although, let's be clear. Compliance is important. You need students to comply with your rules and your requests, such that they produce the work that is required to succeed. So, let's try and summarise. In order to help your students succeed, you need their compliance, which can be gained if you have their respect?

In some classrooms, automatic respect from all is not something you will get. It is something that you have to earn, often over time. In some schools, just being in a school for a number of years gets you a certain level of respect. You are part of the furniture. That gains you a certain level of esteem. Let's presume you are a teacher who has a reputation for helping your students achieve excellent results. That earns you some respect. Let's presume you are a teacher who students feel they can approach if they have a problem. That earns you respect too. Let's presume you are a teacher who is passionate about your subject, and it shows in your lessons. That's right, a little more respect earned. Finally, you treat your students with respect, and value their opinions and contributions (balancing this successfully alongside school rules and dictats from above). Combine all of these together, and you are a teacher who is likely to be respected, leading to students happily complying with your requests. Success?

Well. It isn't as simple as that. Let's add another dimension. No one teacher is the same in terms of style and delivery. Every teacher, whilst trying to be consistent with school rules, will have their own methodology. Following the school behaviour plan consistently only gets you so far. What else can you do, to go that extra mile? To make yourself standout and make your students take notice? For me, it was simple. I simply took my own natural personality, and amplified it within teaching. I have often been referred to as the kindest or 'nicest man in the school' by colleagues, given an unfaltering desire to help others. I dedicate myself completely to my job. Students have referred to me as the teacher who works hardest for them. You need to find out what makes you special as a teacher. What will your students remember you for?

At a basic level, be there to help and support your students. They will respect you, if they know you care and wish to see them succeed. They will value you if they know you will stick around for the long haul. Students are smart. They can read you like a book. More importantly, if you are only there for the pay cheque at the end of the month, and have nothing else to offer, they will see through you. Hence, my belief that teaching is so much more than a 'job'. It is a way of life, a commitment, the ultimate responsibility in shaping the lives of young people. Their future is in your hands. What will you do with it?

14. The Government and ever changing policy

Can you imagine a time when teachers had control over what they taught and how they taught it? In an educational setting far far away, it sounds like teaching in another galaxy. Sounds like paradise. Well, such a time did exist.

Before the National Curriculum was ushered in, teachers had greater autonomy. With the National Curriculum coming down from above in 1988, it signalled what I refer to as the 'top-down era'. One initiative after another, brought down by successive Governments. Or perhaps I only recall history in such a manner, given that I lived through this time period both as a student and then a working teacher.

It could be argued that the National Curriculum is 'national' in scope, thus seemingly ignoring the notion that students are individuals. However, proponents of the National Curriculum would state that teachers can differentiate delivery based on the needs of their students. They would also argue that before the introduction of the National Curriculum, some teachers were not competent enough to deliver a suitable curriculum, hence the need for guidance from above. How much is too much guidance? Guidance on what to teach, how to teach it and how to assess it? This is an argument for another day, and probably an argument that you will explore if you are a PGCE student at university. There are numerous discussions on forums which provide some idea of what life was like before the National Curriculum. Reference: http://goo.gl/bj17tr

Wait. Scrap the paragraph above. If you teach in an academy, you don't have to follow the National Curriculum! You have flexibility. You are free! Yet your curriculum still has to be balanced and broad. What does that mean? Not sure? Is that implying that you may as well take the National Curriculum and deliver it? After all, Ofsted will judge your curriculum implementation. There are no clear answers. Is the freedom afforded to academies really freedom at all?

In my time as a teacher, new 'initiatives' impacting my teaching life have come at me in a constant flow. Changes and initiatives that impact: what I teach (at multiple levels), assessment structures for qualifications, inspection frameworks, league tables, etc. Oh, and let's not forget Government changes to my wages and pension arrangements. Change ahoy!

Then of course, you get a new Government, and more changes are introduced at a whim. Some would certainly argue that changes are introduced without any real long-term plan to measure outcomes.

Changes are introduced, often rapidly, without giving previous initiatives time to sink in. If something is broken, why wipe it out completely? Why not modify it and fix aspects which are broken?

Then you have change for the sake of change - to make a political statement or impression. Some would consider that to be rather irrational. Finally, there is the act of changing things that don't require changing - in order to draw attention away from bigger issues that need addressing. Some would consider that to be disastrous, and all too common in the political arena. Welcome to the glorious world of change.

Change is something you need to keep up with. It is well worth reading up on changes that impact you, and being seriously informed. Also, be wary of upcoming changes which will impact you in a number of years. Whether you agree or disagree with initiatives, you are required to work with them. Ultimately, you are in the business of teaching. You roll with the changing times, adapting as best you can.

15. The stats matter!

What do teachers do? They teach. They prepare for lessons and then deliver those lessons. Resources are created. Work is marked. Reports are written. Parents are contacted. That would seem like the most obvious answer.

However, ultimately, you are judged on how well your classes perform. It could be key stage three students making appropriate progress by the end of years 7, 8 and 9. Year 11, 12 and 13 students achieving their target grade or above.

Ah yes. Target grades. Do you know the target grades of all students you teach? Do you know whether they are on target, below target or above target - at every point during the year? Grades. Results. ALPs scores. League tables. A* to C percentages. Value added. Your school is judged by the results it achieves. A fall in results comparative to previous years or national averages could conceivably trigger an Ofsted inspection.

Your head of department will forever be analysing statistics and recommending interventions to help students achieve a higher grade. There is real pressure on staff to help their students achieve the best grade possible. Not just their target grade, but above their target grade. Interestingly, you may think that the teachers play some role in shaping what those targets grades are. Sadly not. Usually, the grades are determined using prior attainment, plugged into various complex calculations and formulae.

You have probably read criticism in the media, noting how schools are becoming exam factories, interested only in grades, and not doing enough to equip students for working life. Not only working life, but social etiquette and citizenship. The concerns revolve around young people constantly being tested, assessed, tested and assessed again. The pressure placed on them is immense.

However, you can't blame schools for this. Schools understand that many parents will ultimately judge them on GCSE and A Level results. Schools therefore do what is required, in order to maximise those results. The strain placed on teachers however is high. Ultimately, there is no way round this. Unless you opt for teaching in the primary sector, a life in secondary schools will often revolve around maintaining good exam results if you teach key stages four and five.

If your students fail to meet their targets, you will have to explain why. Sometimes there are good reasons, such as illness or absence for extended periods. Regardless, it is always worth keeping a careful note of what interventions you have put into place for individual students, and the impact of those interventions. After all, as their teacher, you are accountable. That is how the system works in many schools, and unless there is a dramatic change in overall culture or direction, this is how it will continue to be.

It will be crucial to maintain appropriate assessment tracking systems, which help you monitor individual student performance accurately throughout the academic year. Any drops in performance should trigger appropriate intervention. If your ICT skills are good, you can create all singing all dancing spreadsheets, which will easily track progress over time, perhaps through using conditional formatting to implement a traffic light system (red, green, amber) to indicate changes in progress. If you are feeling brave, a few IF statements and V Lookup tables can really give you some powerful analysis.

Despite the relentless focus on achieving grades, don't lose sight of why you got into teaching. Perhaps you entered the profession to make a positive difference to the lives of young people, to impart passion for your subject, or to embrace the challenge presented to you. Think back to chapter two, and never lose sight of why you entered the profession to begin with. It is possible to maintain the stats, as well as fulfilling your other goals and reasons for teaching.

16. Rewards used to motivate your classes

Rewards are a powerful tool in your arsenal, acting as a motivator to keep your classroom engine running smoothly. Students may have preferred rewards - for example, a phone call home favoured over a letter that can get lost or misplaced. It is important to grasp the full range of rewards that are available to you. Let's look at a few options.

Praise is perhaps your most basic, but most accessible reward. Praise for the sake of praise is pointless. Genuine praise provided for a reason is meaningful. This will be your most frequently used reward.

Phone calls home are certainly cherished. Direct contact with a parent sends a powerful message. Be aware of some pitfalls. Making a series of phone calls can take longer than you think. Finding a telephone number that works is not easy. Your school system may not be up-to-date. Oh, and most important of all, ensure that you greet parents correctly. Referring to Mrs Robinson as Miss Robinson can lead to awkward exchanges. Phone calls can be used to deliver good news ("Tim has produced an excellent analysis of arctic glaciers") or bad news ("Tim has failed to produce any homework on arctic glaciers for the last three weeks").

Most parents will be grateful for the call, even if it is bad news. Reporting both good and bad news serves as a motivator for students. However, the time of day during which you call can be a point of contention. If nobody picks up at home, you may try the mobile number and catch a parent at work. Unfortunately, if they are busy or rushed, they may not grasp the full extent of your message, and may not even fully grasp which teacher you are! In situations such as this, the home voice mail is a better solution (unless the student gets to the voice mail first and presses delete).

Taking all of this into consideration, you may find that making calls home after 5pm is a more sensible option. However, this assumes that the parent maintains standard 9am to 5pm working hours and so will be home after 5pm. This is a poor assumption to make! Working hours vary widely.

Letters make your reporting of good news (or bad news) seem more 'official', especially if the letter is printed on your school's headed paper. Be wary however, your spelling, punctuation and grammar will need to be top notch! Letters however don't always reach the intended recipient. It is not uncommon for students to get home first and hide (or dispose of) the mail. In this situation, a phone call is superior to a letter.

Postcards are a great tool in your arsenal, since they are quick to complete (if your admin department will kindly write out the student addresses). Postcards can be purchased online, although good quality postcards can be quite expensive.

If your school has the appropriate systems and infrastructure in place, then text messages are very convenient. The message goes directly to the parents, reporting good or bad news. Again, the reporting of both can serve to be a motivator. There are two assumptions to make here. Firstly, you assume that the parent has provided a mobile number to the school. Secondly, you assume that they read their text messages (or know how to).

Some parents will provide e-mail addresses. This can be a convenient method of contact. However, your e-mail etiquette needs to be perfect. Use a suitable subject header. Also, ensure your greeting and closing is appropriate. For example, using the word 'Hi' may not be appropriate. 'Dear' may be better. There is one major pitfall with e-mails. Let's pretend that a parent provides an e-mail address at the start of the year, utilising a free e-mail provider. It is feasible to assume that the parent may stop checking that e-mail account. We all have free e-mail accounts that we create and then conveniently forget about when we sign up with another provider. At the very least, assume that e-mail accounts won't be checked every day.

Food. An expensive reward to consider. I have witnessed milkshake parties in action. I have smelt pizza parties. Chocolate. Cake. Muffins. Sweets. The list of potential food rewards is endless. Be careful though! Students will have allergies. You could reward a student with a chocolate bar you deem to be safe, but then have to call an ambulance. Were you aware of their nut allergy? This could land you in serious trouble. Food is therefore quite a risky reward. Check your school's data on student allergies. I have used food as a reward for older students in the past. Get your coursework done on time, and perhaps there is a triple chocolate muffin waiting for you. If you really want to surprise students, fruit is a great reward. They hate it. Yet, we do have a responsibility to promote healthy eating!

Let's finish with a simple reward. Recognition. Having a poster in your classroom entitled 'student of the week' is a simple yet powerful tool. Each week, a different name is written on the poster. Students thrive on recognition of their talents and abilities. We all do. We are human after all. Perhaps a poster for each year group? Or a poster for each class? Gold stars next to names works just as well - even for the older students! Finally, consider the use of school assemblies. Reading out a few names in recognition of good quality work can sometimes be just as effective as a lengthy phone call or an expensive triple chocolate muffin. Be aware however, that some students are very self-conscious, and won't always appreciate a shout-out in front of their peers. Therefore, try to discern which types of reward are preferred by different students, and act accordingly.

Do be aware that all students deserve recognition for their efforts. All students deserve your time. There is a temptation to focus your efforts on motivating students who display poor behaviour or weak ability, they may require a much larger proportion of your time and support. However, it is important not to get 'swamped'. Do ensure that all students get your attention at one point or another.

A lot has been written about motivation, engaging students, and the utilisation of rewards, and the psychology behind it. I have only scratched the surface, offering you a summary of techniques that have worked well for me over the years. This is an area that you will certainly want to research further.

17. Going beyond the academic curriculum

Resilience. Cooperation. Independence. These are all skills that students should be developing and demonstrating in your lessons. You can add critical thinking, creativity and leadership to the list too. In the long run, helping your students to demonstrate these skills will probably do just as much (if not more) to prepare them for the world of work, as preparing them for exams.

You can develop resilience by setting tasks that are achievable yet challenging, and which encourage students not to give up. These tasks should set a level of challenge which force students to think carefully, as opposed to providing easy answers quickly. An initial temporary stumbling block on a task may encourage students to think harder or more widely. In solving a challenging task, you can then encourage both independent learning as well as cooperation through group work. Hopefully, as your students put further thought into the task, engagement with the task increases, drumming up a real sense of enthusiasm in wanting to see the task through to completion. The students then take pride in the end result. Pride in not only the work they have produced, but taking pride in having overcome a challenge.

Critical thinking may be harder to encourage. Most GCSE and A Level specifications will call for critical thinking in some guise. However, large proportions of some GCSE and A Level specifications are still based on the constant reproduction of pre-practised techniques or factual recall, i.e. a timed memory test. Therefore, there can be an obsession with memorising your notes in time for an exam, as opposed to applying your knowledge critically.

Regardless, you can still build in critical thinking into your lesson delivery. You can encourage your students to think critically about how to solve a problem, evaluating different methods of achieving the solution. Once the solution is achieved, which method was the most efficient and why? Students can also think critically about a topic area using evaluative language, or focus on evaluating what is good and bad about a particular piece of work. From this, students can then raise appropriate questions about a piece of work, acknowledging different viewpoints or opinions.

In terms of creativity, is there an opportunity for students think of creative solutions to problems? Can you encourage them to think outside of the box, finding alternate methods to solve a problem, as opposed to relying on prescribed methods suggested by the text book (or a teacher)?

Leadership can be easily demonstrated and encouraged through group tasks. It is important for students to understand what leadership means, and what a leader is responsible for in relation to the task. Preparation for a group presentation is a perfect chance to assess leadership skills - not only for the group leader, but for the other group members as well. Various parts of the task may well allow for each member of the group to demonstrate some form of leadership and forward thinking.

18. Form tutor expectations

Consider this scenario. As an NQT, you escaped having a form group. You do the odd bit of support, but mostly you have been left to your own devices. It is the last day of the Autumn term. School breaks up tomorrow, and then it is Christmas. You check your inbox one last time before departing on Friday afternoon. A new e-mail has arrived. The subject header simply says 'January 9F'. Should you open it, or leave it? You have a plane to catch, your holiday awaits! Curiosity gets the better of you. You open it. The e-mail is short and very much to the point. You are now the replacement form tutor for 9F. A million thoughts race through your head. The plane can wait. You look up 9F's student list and hit print. The printer is out of paper. Great. You run off looking for the head of year.

You return from the Christmas holiday. It is AM registration. You walk up to the classroom. It says '9F' on the door. You walk through the door. You don't know what to expect, but there is no time for regrets. No time to look back. The room quietens, and thirty faces stare expectantly at you.

Back to reality. Being a form tutor is one of the most pivotal roles in any school. You undertake basic tasks such as completing registers (a legal requirement) and overseeing uniform standards, as well as having more complex responsibilities (mentor, role model, motivator, psychologist, therapist). Preparation is essential. Know your form group. Know how to support each student in the group. Understand their needs.

Let's run through daily routines. Each day of the week, you will want an activity that your form group can engage with. Your school will likely have an agreed structure already in place.

For example, Monday could be reading. Yes, that's right, encouraging students to read. Some will do no reading at home. Some will only read what is given to them at school. See if you can extend their minds. Explain to them the importance of reading, and the part it will play in shaping their lives later. Of course, they will be expecting you to say this. So turn the situation on its head. Give the usual speech on how important reading is for developing their vocabulary, which will aid them later in life, etc. Then, catch their attention. What have you (the teacher) read recently? Fiction? Non-fiction? Why did you read it? Why did you find it so interesting?

Many of the students will have seen films based on books. Take a popular film. Show them a scene from the film. Link this to a chapter in the book. Use the book to bring alive the world portrayed by the film.

The power of writing to transport you away, into a completely different world, allowing you suspend disbelief, if only for a short time. Some students will appreciate your efforts, and won't need much more convincing. Other students will need much more convincing.

Your next strategy is to link their reading to their interests. If they like football, has their favourite footballer released an autobiography? You get the idea. If the students don't own any of these books at home, can your school library source them? Alternatively, there is the idea of reading on tablets, Kindles or phones. Although, this will depend on your school's policy!

On Tuesday, perhaps you go through the news. How many of your students will watch the news (or read the news) on a daily basis? How many are aware of key events going on around them? Some students will express boredom when confronted with the news. Then it is up to you to make it interesting. Pick a story that you know will interest them, and then surround this with a couple of other stories which are deemed important. Hopefully by the end of the year, they will have a strong knowledge of key events, which are economic, political, social, cultural and technological in nature. Most students will take an interest if you explain clearly how an event will impact their lives. For example, if VAT goes up, that impacts their ability to buy designer trainers, which become more expensive! Link the story to their daily lives and interests. Soon, you will have an eager audience.

Wednesday may consist of diary signing. This is where you check each diary and look for a parent signature. The idea being that the parent has checked the diary before signing it. You then countersign. Each school will have its own system. Consider what you would do if a student has not had their diary signed?

Thursday may consist of private study. Students get on with something relevant to aid their learning. It could be revision for an upcoming test, group revision, extending an activity from class, etc.

Friday may well be assembly day. Whatever happens, ensure you are on time to assembly with your form group. Being late is embarrassing. Forgetting to go to assembly is shocking.

So, Monday to Friday, your form group is occupied. Why complete activities during form time? It is all about setting routines. If students know what to expect when they walk through the door, it makes your life easier and their lives easier. Set routines and set expectations right from the very beginning. This is absolutely crucial. A good set of routines to start the day is also likely to get students into the right frame of mind, such that lesson one gets off to a good start. The teacher of lesson one will thank you!

As a form tutor, you will also contact parents (sometimes, it will be contacting the same parents on a regular basis). You have lots to talk about. For example, Tim needs to come to school in the right shoes. Mary needs to get the five rings removed from her nose. Tom's attendance is poor, he was absent for three days earlier this week. You will want to find out why he was absent and try to get some assurances that attendance will improve. Harry was late to school each day this week, why was he late and what can be done to improve his punctuality? Joe's performance in Maths, Science and History has not been good, his reports have shown that he is underperforming significantly and not completing homework.

After phoning or writing home, if issues can't be resolved, you may wish to conduct a meeting. You would invite parents in, have any other relevant teachers present, and try and work out a solution. Meetings can be very time consuming to setup and undertake. However, their value is immense. The act of personally meeting a parent face to face has a different effect, compared to merely talking to them over the phone or writing to them via e-mail. The head of year may be present in the meeting, or may even run the meeting.

After each termly report is released, I have always found it useful to store report data on each tutee, looking to track patterns over time. This can then be used to inform mini interviews, where you have a chance to discuss academic progress (or the lack of it). You can set targets and then monitor outcomes. This can be used to inform purposeful contact home.

A key area of responsibility for a form tutor is to monitor student welfare. Keep your eyes open. Look out for issues, relating to neglect (physical and mental). If you see anything of concern, or hear anything of concern, you will want to take action. Usually, this will involve reporting the issue to someone in your pastoral hierarchy. You will want to talk to students as well, to gather more information. The process of doing this is a delicate one. Your school should provide appropriate training.

PSHCEE. Citizenship. Some form tutors dread teaching this. Your school will probably provide you with a scheme of work. Politics. The law. Drugs education. Sex education. Relationships. Handling money and finances. Careers. Human rights and equality. Some schools have one hour per week that is set for delivering PSHCEE to form groups. Other schools will utilise a rolling one hour timetable. So PSHCEE is delivered Monday period one, and then Monday period two the following week, and so on. Often you will find yourself needing to put significant time into preparing these lessons.

Or, you could get lucky and find yourself in a school where Citizenship teachers are employed to deliver what is required. Regardless, you have a key responsibility as far as helping your tutees develop into positive citizens. Essentially, that starts with you being a good role model, even before you start teaching them anything.

Being a form tutor is incredibly rewarding. This chapter has given you a taste of what is to be expected. You have the opportunity to get to know your students, to develop positive routines and structures, which allow for the smooth running of the school. You see the students each morning. Therefore, you will find that you know the students better than some other members of staff that teach them. Consequently, you will find yourself intervening on behalf of other teachers. You may carry your form group over several years. Students crave stability, and will therefore welcome your presence year after year. Due to the relationship you develop, students will place a strong level of trust in you. Hence being a form tutor is an incredible position of responsibility. Use the power you have wisely. As a form tutor, you can truly make a significant difference.

19. The school engine

You probably read the chapter title and thought what on earth is he going on about now? The school engine? Every school has an engine. It's what keeps the school running. Without the engine, the school can't move forward. It's no different to a car.

Picture this scenario. It is Monday morning, 7.30am. It's cold. It's dark. It's snowing. You park your car and notice the premises staff shovelling snow and laying down salt. You enter the school, trying not to slip over. You get into your classroom. Someone has turned on the heating hours ago. The school is cosy and warm.

You turn on your PC and find it has the dreaded blue screen of death (BSOD). You run to the IT technicians in a panic. They smile and understand. Minutes later they have replaced your PC. You are thankful. You load up your resources for period one and then exit in a hurry.

You go past the reprographics room to pick up your photocopied worksheets. The reprographics staff have provided the thirty copies, double-sided, stapled and hole punched, with the first page in colour as requested. You dash past your classroom, depositing your worksheets in the appropriate tray.

On the way to assembly, you run into the exams officer, who gives you the upcoming summer exam entries for checking. She has already checked them, but needs you to double check.

Lessons start for the day. You get through the first two periods without incident. Your learning support assistants were incredibly helpful. Period three however presents a problem. A student has a never-ending nosebleed. Your remaining supply of tissues is exhausted, before you send the student to the welfare room with a note. The welfare assistant sends the student back within minutes, right as rain.

Period three ends and it is break time. A break for you? Never! More running around. Your classroom door handle has come loose. A quick call to reception and the premises staff are alerted. Within seconds, someone appears with a drill and your door is fixed.

Period four is a free period. A 'free' period for you? There is no such thing. The receptionist phones you and informs you that your visitor is here. Thankfully the meeting doesn't last very long. Thirty minutes left of period four, time for some quick marking. An e-mail comes through from one of the admin staff. They have sent out your letters.

The end of period four signals lunch time. Food! You hurry down to the canteen, greeted politely by the canteen staff. A small wink, and they serve you a bigger portion of shepherd's pie, with extra custard in your pudding. You are thankful. This will help you get through period five.

Period five. This is what you were dreading all day. You are covering an Art lesson. You know nothing about art. You don't even remember learning the subject at school. You can't paint. You can't draw. Thankfully, the art technician steps in and helps out. Soon all of the students are busy working away, and the technician steps out. You are grateful. Saved from disaster.

It is 3pm. The end of the day. Peace and bliss! Wrong. Time for an endless stream of meetings. The admin staff have kindly provided tea, coffee and a wide selection of biscuits. Biscuits? That gets everyone's attention. There is a mad rush to the biscuit tray. You gather up three chocolate biscuits and retreat.

It is 5pm. The meetings are over. You have an hour to get some marking and planning done. You are desperate not to take any work home tonight. It is 6.30pm. The premises staff are locking up. Not wanting to be an inconvenience, you offer to leave. They take pity on your stressed and dishevelled state. They give you an extra ten minutes to finish your work. A kind gesture.

The scenario above sounds like a reflection of a teacher's busy day. Teachers do more than just teach. Actually, it is not a reflection of your busy day. Well, it is. Just not in the context of this chapter. The scenario illustrates very clearly how you have been helped by a variety of other staff during the day:

1) premises staff

2) IT technicians

3) reprographics staff

4) exams officer

5) learning support assistant

6) welfare assistant

7) reception staff

8) admin staff

9) canteen staff

10) art, science and design technology technicians

These staff have helped you to function. They are the school engine. Without them you would have nothing. They work hard just like you, but behind the scenes, and often for less pay. Yet they show up to work, and do the best they can. Be kind to them. Be grateful to them. If possible reciprocate the support and help them out when you can.

20. Unions, strikes, pay and retirement

You are lucky to be working in a profession which has a strong union presence. Joining a union is certainly in your best interests. Yes, their yearly fee doesn't come cheap. However, you never know when you will need their support. They are very much a safety net for teachers.

Sometimes, I do wonder what my yearly fee pays for. I seem to get no end of mail from my union, often promoting sales literature from third party companies. Most of those letters and leaflets go straight into the bin. Occasionally, something useful will come through.

Unions also promote action during desperate times. Recent strike action over pay, workload and pension arrangements suggests that teachers are willing to make a stand. Is this stand justified? Certainly it is. Teacher pay has suffered under recent austerity measures, with pay freezes and below inflation rises. Living on a teacher's salary is not easy. Working in this profession certainly isn't about making money (unlike some other professions). However, a teacher deserves to be paid a reasonable wage. After all, is it not reasonable to assume that a teacher should find it affordable to live in the local area of their school? For example, a teacher who works in a London school should find it affordable to live in London.

I have known a number of teachers who have moved out of London, simply because they can't afford to pay the cost of living in London. This would potentially suggest that over time, schools in London are losing out on some of the best teachers. Given the pivotal role that teachers play in shaping the future of a nation, you would think that the Government would address their concerns with a little more urgency.

The trouble with union strike action, is that each strike tends to be a one-off event. Some schools will close completely. Some schools will remain manned by a small number of staff, and will open doors to a selected number of year groups. Currently, it seems that strike action appears to have no real impact in terms of sending a strong message to the Government. At worst, it is one day of inconvenience for parents. Whether you are for or against strike action, one thing is clear. Unions need to re-evaluate how they engage with the Government to get their message across. They need to do more to make themselves heard. Two strikes per year doesn't seem to have done much over the last few years, in terms of getting the Government to take notice.

If you enter the teaching profession, you need to be aware that you may well be taken for granted. Your school, colleagues and management may appreciate what you do. However, despite the mission critical nature of your job in terms of educating and developing the young minds which will be the future of this country, other stakeholders may not value your efforts as much. Dwelling on that thought for a while, injects a dose of reality into one's worldview. Therefore sometimes, it is important to put those thoughts to one side, and get on with the job at hand.

You need to consider retirement. You need to think about when you will retire and what arrangements you have in place. Ensure you have pension provision available, either through the Teachers' Pensions scheme or some other private scheme. Your retirement age was once 60. That makes sense, when you consider the physical and mental toll that teaching takes on your body. You are on your feet for up to six hours of the day, teaching challenging classes, who will sap your physical and mental energy. Teaching in a demanding school whilst going through the twilight years of your career is not easy.

Well, let's cheer everyone up a bit. The retirement age is no longer 60. If you are new to the profession, your retirement will likely rise in line with the state pension age. So 68 is a more likely age for retirement (depending on a number of factors that your union or the Teachers' Pension service can advise you on). One can only presume that 70 will be on the cards soon. It is important that you do your own reading and research into this area. When you read this book, conditions, rules and regulations may well have changed (again). For further information, go to: https://www.teacherspensions.co.uk/

Indeed, this is a rather depressing chapter. Let's not dwell on this. Let's move on and consider something a little more enlightening.

21. That theory is useful!

Over the years, beginner teachers have often said to me that they don't understand why they have to sit through lectures at university. Common complaints have often revolved around theory not relating to everyday practice.

But don't dismiss that theory. It is there to be applied. What was covered may help you when you least expect it. A strategy you learn about today, may help you next year. So don't fall asleep during lectures.

Whilst undertaking my PGCE course, I recall a lecture on meeting the needs of EAL students. Yet, there were no EAL students in the classes I was teaching. However, in my second placement school, there were lots of EAL students. Suddenly, that theory became useful. Those notes I took become a lifesaver. If you are a PGCE student, then this is your opportunity to try things out. Trial and error. Apply the theory into the classroom, and see what happens. Reshape your delivery based on the outcomes.

This chapter is very much short and sweet. As a PGCE student, the simple message is absorb everything you can from university. If you are an NQT or part of the Teach First or School Direct programme, collect anything useful from INSET sessions in your school. Get it all down on paper at least. Don't dismiss it because it may not be useful today at this very moment. Save it for a rainy day, and then apply into your teaching practice when needed.

22. Be yourself (*or my excuse for a story*)

A strange chapter heading. 'Be yourself'. What does it mean? Before we proceed, this chapter is probably most useful for new teachers undertaking their PGCE year, having yet to decide on a particular teaching style that suits them.

Over the years, I have witnessed some trainee teachers go through a difficult process. They notice a problem in one of their classes and change their approach accordingly. Initially, this sounds fine. However, they may put great efforts into transforming themselves into something completely different. Why such a radical transformation? Well, there is pressure to be something more than they currently are. Pressure to be something different, in the hope it leads to success. Pressure to produce results quickly. That transformation doesn't always work out. It becomes hard to maintain. I would liken it to the world of fantasy - acting like a dragon, when one is actually a goblin (or vice versa). Let me try and explain.

The dragon breathes fire. The dragon is strong and dominant. The dragon usually has a situation under control. The dragon however is proud and arrogant to a fault. It isn't very agile in all situations, and one can easily see and hear it coming. However, it has ruled by fear for hundreds of years, and so the villagers fall into line. They know that a dragon is never to be messed with!

The goblin finds daily life a little more challenging. The goblin knows that it has a skill set which is unique and useful - it is more agile than the dragon and is better at anticipating future problems that may arise. The goblin is a better negotiator. However, people don't always listen to the goblin. The goblin is sometimes overpowered. The goblin has to shout a little louder to be heard. However, once it has the attention of the audience, it is in control.

One day, in a fit of envy, the goblin decides that it wants to be a dragon. Being a dragon must make life so much easier. Using magic, the goblin successfully disguises its appearance. It appears as a dragon, breathing fire and flame. Suddenly, it is unstoppable. What an incredible feeling. Always in control. No obstructions. The villagers of all surrounding lands surrender immediately. However, the spell was only temporary. The goblin could not maintain the facade. Generating all of that fire was not easy and really took a toll on the goblin's health. Soon, the villagers saw through the disguise. They were not happy. The goblin was embarrassed.

Fleeing in fear, the goblin approached the real dragon for advice. The dragon laughed at the goblin and exclaimed, "You should never try to be something you are not. You don't see me prancing around in the shadows, adept at negotiation and cunning. No, I am a dragon. I breathe fire. Everyone fears me. It's what I am. It's what I do."

As a teacher, you may feel pressured into being someone you are not. You may look around at other teachers, noting their successful teaching styles. You may read guidance on best practice, which dictates how you should teach. Four observers watch you teach and give you advice:

1) "You should be like Mr Smith. He has perfect control of his classes. He is the scariest teacher in the school. You can hear him shouting down the corridor. Nobody dares confront or question him! Every lesson starts off with a stern lecture on manners and values!"

2) "You should be like Mrs Simpson. She runs around the classroom a mile a minute. Her teaching moves at such an incredible pace, the students don't have time to misbehave!"

3) "You should be like Mr Wells. He is so calm in every situation. He never loses his cool. All disruptive situations are diffused in an expert manner. I have never heard him raise his voice. He makes it look so easy."

4) "You should be like Mr Jones. He starts each of his lessons with a song and a dance. Last week, he was explaining the periodic table through rapping. The students loved it! Let's not forget him playing his guitar at the last parents evening. The parents all wanted to meet him."

So what should you do? Which of the four approaches should you go with? No particular style or approach is necessarily correct. Ask yourself this very important question: what style do you feel comfortable delivering? Trying to imitate Mr Smith could be disastrous for your vocal cords. Trying to imitate Mrs Simpson could lead to a trip to hospital based on exhaustion. Trying to imitate Mr Jones could end badly if you can't sing, dance or rap. Embarrassment and a loss of confidence may well be the end result. Finally, we are left with Mr Wells. Sounds ideal doesn't it. Being calm in every situation. Perfect control. However, that often takes time and practice to build up. Mr Wells probably did not get there overnight.

Mr Smith, Mrs Simpson, Mr Wells and Mr Jones all promote different traits. They all have different styles - or at least styles they have become stereotyped against. In other words, you only hear half the story.

Mr Smith is strict and scary. That's not the only defining aspect of his teaching style. There is so much more he brings to the table, that doesn't get reported or discussed. He is also good at understanding why some students behave poorly. He works hard to resolve those underlying causes by working closely with parents and outside agencies.

Mrs Simpson may have incredibly well paced lessons, but she also provides feedback to students that is easily digested and rewards students for their efforts, making them feel truly valued. All students feel that they can achieve and make progress in her classes.

Mr Jones may be known for his singing and dancing, but he always makes it very clear to students why the subject content they are learning is important, and how it impacts on daily life. He makes his subject relevant and engaging.

Mr Wells is calm in all situations. However, he also laid out his expectations very clearly at the start of the year. He treats his students with respect, expecting the same in return. He made it clear that his objective is to see them succeed, and they must work together in partnership to enable this to happen.

Mr Smith, Mrs Simpson, Mr Wells and Mr Jones all have reputations built up over many years. They are part of the furniture. Your best solution is to learn from all of them. Apply what you can from each of them, and then develop your own teaching style. Trying to imitate one teacher entirely will probably lead to failure in the long run. Look at your personality. Look at your key strengths. Use your strengths to hide your weaknesses. Use this as a launching point, and you will be fine.

The key to success is invoking a style which you are fully comfortable with. You have to feel in control and confident as far as your delivery is concerned. A failure to be confident will show immediately. The students will pick up on it, and it will only make things worse. As the chapter heading implies, be yourself.

Let's assume that you go through your PGCE year, having developed your preferred style. Fantastic. You feel confident and satisfied. Nothing more to do? Umm, actually, it's not over. It is now the start of your NQT year. Your style is fine for class 9a on Monday morning. However, soon you notice that it is not appropriate for class 9c on a Friday after lunch. An observer of class 9c may recommend drastic changes, pointing to things that are not going well. That same observer may not have seen you teach any of your other classes.

Look into how you can adapt your style. What small changes can you make which will make the biggest difference? For example, perhaps the answer lies in how you start the lesson off. A visual starter activity, rather than a written activity? A change to how students enter the room? Can these small changes help the class settle more quickly?

You will probably find that a complete overhaul of your style may not be the answer. What makes 9c different to 9a, and why? Once you figure this out, your life becomes so much easier.

Each class has different students with different needs. Using one fixed style that doesn't change is not really going to work. I would therefore recommend one overarching style which works for you, but with changes made as required depending on what each class needs. How do you discover what changes are needed? Well, the process of reflection may help. More on reflection in the next chapter.

23. Reflection

Do you know what it means to reflect on something? What is the last thing you reflected on in your life? All of us will attribute a slightly different meaning to reflection. I suppose we all reflect in different ways. Regardless, after reflecting on something, are we brave enough to take action if something is not right?

Look back over everything you have read so far in regards to organisation, planning, managing health, using technology, managing your students and teaching styles. Can you reflect on how your reading impacts on your desired teaching style? What does your reflection reveal? Has anything you have read in this book caused you to think differently about how you teach (or why you teach)? Has anything in this book provided a solution to a problem you may have?

Regardless of how you view the process of reflection, it is important to know that reflection is essential. You need to be reflecting constantly on your teaching, carefully reviewing your lesson delivery and assessment practice. You should also reflect on your effective use of technology and your approach to engaging each of your classes. Each class is likely to need a slightly different approach, allowing you to cater for the diverse range of student personalities. Does your teaching allow you to account for the needs of every student in each class? If not, what can you do to allow for this?

> Learn from the past.
> Evaluate the present.
> Shape the future.

If reshaping your practice based on reflection doesn't go to plan, try again. Don't be afraid of getting things wrong. Learn from past mistakes and see how you can improve.

A journal or diary may help you. Writing things down or keeping a record of key events allows you to see progress made (or not made) over time. If you teach lots of different classes, noting down your reflections on what works or doesn't work with each class may be helpful. This also allows you to cross-reference strategies between classes. Through this process, you may discover that what works for class 8d may also work for 8f.

Whilst you may undertake your own personal reflection, consider using others to help the process along. Student surveys can be helpful, where you ask students what could be improved in your lessons. Students will appreciate the opportunity to help shape their lessons. Also, they may reveal something that colleagues or inspectors miss. After all, a lesson observation carried out by a colleague is nothing more than a snapshot, which may not be a true reflection of usual practice.

Reflect not just on the process of teaching, but also on your 'happiness'. Are you happy in your current school? Are you happy as a teacher. What can make your teaching life more enjoyable?

You should also encourage your students to reflect. Do you give them time to reflect in lessons? Having assessed their work and reflected on the quality of it, are they satisfied with the effort they have put in? What else can your students reflect on, apart from the quality of their work? As a form tutor, you could encourage your students to keep a reflective diary or journal.

Teachers and students are often too busy to reflect. There is always something that needs doing, either in our teaching life or our personal life. As a result, the process of reflection may get neglected or pushed aside. Alternatively, if things are not going well, you may be scared to reflect, finding any excuse possible to delay the process. In this situation, reflecting alongside someone else who you trust may be helpful.

24. Give it time

This chapter is aimed primarily at PGCE trainees. The previous chapter on reflection mentioned that you should not be afraid to make mistakes, providing you can learn from them and move on. Over the last few months, I have become far more active on Twitter, counselling trainee teachers. A key worry is a fear of making mistakes or not having a class perfect from day one. As teachers, we age like wine - i.e. we get better over time. Year after year, you pick up new techniques, new tricks, new hints, and smarter ways of working. Consider yourself to be a puzzle. As time goes by, the pieces slowly come together. However, you are never truly complete, since you never stop learning. Always refining and changing your practice.

To expect a trainee teacher to be as refined and polished as an experienced teacher from day one is unrealistic. So if you start your training and find yourself struggling with certain aspects of the job, don't worry. Put strategies into place to address your concerns, and try different things.

Don't be afraid to ask for help. It is not an admission of weakness. Pride should be forgotten. It is important to remember why we are here. We are here to teach. We are here to aid our students in their progression through the schooling process. We are here because of the students. So, it is imperative that we do everything we can for them. If re-evaluating how we teach and what we teach is going to benefit the students, then so be it.

Hopefully, you have landed in a supportive school, where staff can help you through the process. A supportive group of staff is the key to success (in a training environment, or a 'real' teaching environment). If you can trust your fellow staff and rely on them for support, you will find your training placements so much easier. Supportive staff may not only provide you with constructive feedback on lessons, but also act as a reassuring and sympathetic presence, giving you the time and opportunities required to grow. If such support is absent in your school, it does make your placement more difficult. If you are unlucky enough to find yourself in such an environment, do ask your university tutor for help. Sometimes, simple misunderstandings can be smoothed over very quickly.

If things are not perfect in the first few weeks (or months), don't worry. It will all come together, providing you are able to act on feedback and advice. A log of strategies that you have tried with different classes will help immensely. This will allow you track what has worked and what hasn't worked, ensuring you don't repeat techniques which were of no value. You may think a log is overkill. However, when you have a dozen classes, perhaps on a rotating fortnightly timetable, your memory will become hazy.

If things are problematic, consider asking your university tutor to come in for additional visits. Given their experience gained from visiting a large variety of schools, they may offer you a perspective that is outside of the box.

It is worth considering what you are ultimately pursing. You want your students to give you their attention (and their respect). How you go about obtaining that is up to you. There is no standard answer. However, as boring as it sounds, following school rules and behaviour policies consistently (alongside other staff) is a great start. Everything else will hopefully slot into place with time and experience.

In a year or two, consider putting your experiences and knowledge to good use through doing your own research and publishing your findings. Shared knowledge is power after all. That is something the teaching profession as a whole isn't great at. How many academic teaching journals do you read? Do you have access to any teaching journals? Have you ever heard of a teaching journal? If you are a trainee, you will have access to journals through your university, and will probably utilise them for your assignments.

Beyond utilising journals for your assignments (seen by some as a long and laborious process), use them to help your own practice (certainly a very useful and fulfilling practice). Search for articles of interest. Most teachers who are embedded in schools won't have access to these journals - unless their school holds a subscription. Given the immense cost, that is highly unlikely. So whilst you are a trainee attached to a university, take advantage of what journals can offer you. Unlike books, journals will give you access to the latest and cutting edge experience and practice. Yes, it involves doing more reading. Yes, that is time consuming. Yet, you never know what you will find that could be of value. When your training is over, access to journals is likely to disappear. So take advantage of them while you can.

25. Life after teaching

I have discussed life after teaching in a previous chapter. However, it is critical enough to warrant its own chapter.

How long do you plan to teach for? This is a valid question that you need to ask yourself. Do you plan on teaching until you are 68? Or do you have an exit plan? This is not a question that enough teachers think about. The temptation is to only think of tomorrow or next week. Thinking about next month, next year or the next decade lacks any sense of urgency.

Can you see yourself as a head teacher? Or are you content to be a classroom teacher, head of department, head of year, assistant head or deputy head? After you have taught for a number of years and obtained the promotion that you desire, do you plan to keep heading up that ladder? Whatever your 'final' role is, how long do you wish to remain in that role? Something to keep in mind for the future.

Have you considered working for a university? Lecturing in your subject at a higher level does have a very different feel to teaching in a secondary (or primary) classroom. Perhaps you would venture towards becoming an author? After a number of years in the classroom, your experience will certainly make you qualified to publish books or resources on areas that you feel you are competent in.

The planning process for your future is very much a personal process. Try and balance financial need with a desire to do what you enjoy. You really need to start thinking about the future as soon as possible. Lay down as much groundwork as you can. You will thank yourself in a few years! The message is simple. Think now. Be ready to act later.

26. Wider challenges

This chapter considers some of the wider challenges that impact your students' engagement with education on a daily basis. Perhaps the better term to use is 'factors'. Some of these factors can't really be 'solved' or fully addressed in the short term, and may be out of your immediate control. Regardless, I do believe that they have some influence on learning in your classroom. Even if you feel that the impact on your students is minimal, it is certainly worth having an awareness of what they are about.

Stability of the family unit

Firstly, let's consider how society has changed over the last few decades. This change I am referring to is in terms of the family unit. At school, students crave stability. This is achieved through the use of routines (even though they may initially grumble) and knowing what to expect. At home, it is similar. Yet, obviously, at home there is a deep emotional attachment. It is no secret that divorce rates have been on the rise in recent decades. This does have an impact on your students. If the family unit breaks apart, it can be very difficult for students to cope mentally. This becomes evident through changes in behaviour and changes in personality. Some students are more adversely impacted compared to others.

If you come to know about changes in a student's family life, the best that you can do is be supportive wherever possible. You also want to be conscious when phoning or writing home, being aware of how this can further impact the family dynamic and the student's mindset.

Culture at home

One would hope that parents will do everything in their power to support their children through the schooling process. Part of that involves encouraging their children to engage with education, but also providing a suitable environment that is conducive to the completion of school work or educational activities. This can mean monitoring what their children do at key times, setting appropriate time limits on activities, and ensuring rules are enforced. Sounds simple. It isn't.

What would your response be if a parent said: "Tom goes to his games console when he is home from school. We get home by 7pm and convince him to do an hour of homework, then he watches television whilst eating dinner alone." It would be interesting to ponder how common a scenario this is in current society.

For some of your students, they will spend a large proportion of their time alone at home. Alone does not have to mean home alone. It can simply mean not being supervised by an adult, or an adult not having an idea of what their child is up to. Either that, or they will be out with friends. In a worst case scenario, basic rules are not enforced at home and boundaries are constantly crossed. That assumed stability may not exist. Teachers are quick to blame poor parenting. Can you blame a parent who is having to work incredibly long hours to make ends meet, and therefore struggles to spend quality time with their children?

For some students, school life is the only stable structure they will experience. Be aware of that when you teach students who can't understand why you are trying to impose rules and boundaries.

Diet

What do your students eat and drink on the way to school? What do they eat and drink at lunch time? A morning pre-school visit to the local newsagents will allow for them to stock up on fizzy drinks and sweets. Not just one drink. Not just one chocolate bar. A school bag full of ultra-sized fizzy drink bottles. Where do they get the money from to buy all of these items? Where does self-control come in, as far as deciding how much to buy? Is it safe to assume that the overconsumption of sugary food and drinks during the school day negatively impacts learning? I will let you do your own reading and draw your own conclusions. Some schools have banned the consumption of certain sugary drinks, under the impression that learning is impeded. More importantly, if you are concerned about a student's diet during the school day, how responsive will parents be if you make contact?

We have touched on the consumption of food at school. Something further to consider is what your students eat at home. Oily fish, whole grains, fruit, vegetables and nuts. Do parents have the knowledge (and available funding) to provide their children with a balanced nutritious diet? If the answer is no, what solutions exist? Some schools will provide breakfast clubs, aimed at targeting students who would benefit the most from an improved diet. Yet the constraint that appears again is funding.

The health eating agenda has been pushed for years. Yet, when push comes to shove, if a child passes a shop on the way to school and spends all of their pocket money on sugary drinks because they like the taste, who is going to stop them and monitor what they consume?

Social networking

I touched on social networking in an earlier chapter, discussing the need for students to follow social networking etiquette. I don't want to repeat much of what was said before. Conflicts that start online and then extend their way into the classroom can be resolved by a proactive head of year and pastoral team. Regardless, the poor navigation of social networking by students is going to continue to be a hindrance for schools.

Part of the problem revolves around adults themselves not being great role models. All you have to do is visit a forum on your favourite hobby or interest, and note the harsh words and critical language used by many users. At times, the nature of language and communication is truly shocking. The use of language which would never be used in an open face-to-face conversation, yet is thrown around openly online. The assumption being that the user can hide behind their computer screen.

To exemplify this situation, popular social networking platforms have acknowledged online bullying to be an issue and have provided clearer guidelines and rules on tackling abusive language. Yet, what is to stop someone from simply creating a new account and then continuing to misuse social media?

Given the uncontrolled and very much unregulated nature of the online world, what hope do young people have when engaging with social media? We talk of role models needing to be present in the family home and role models being needed in wider society. We also need role models online. I am not sure how that would work, but the current approach isn't working.

Changes in popular culture

Here, I am referring simply to changes in media and entertainment - channelled through television, music, video games and the internet. What was once unacceptable is now acceptable. Have young people (and society in general) been able to process all of this? A common topic of discussion in staffrooms is how young people have less respect today, and how they are far more liberal with their use of language. Where did it all go wrong you will hear teachers moan. Television, video games and music will often receive the blame. There's too much violence! There's too much foul language! It is very easy and convenient to imply that all of this has negatively influenced how your students conduct themselves. Let's take a step back and look into my childhood.

I grew up in the 1980s and early 1990s as a pro wrestling fan. Wrestling shown on national television in both the USA and UK was considered to be a family friendly product. This was in-line with expectations at the time. Television in general was reasonably tame. Extreme violence, rude language and sexualised content was only shown post-watershed and in limited quantities (on subscription channels). Generally, television networks in both the USA and UK took a cautious approach.

In the mid to late 1990s, I remember feeling that something had changed. Something was different! The wrestling was no longer the family friendly product of decades past. It had transformed, with a very liberal and frequent use of rude language, alongside other decadent content. One could argue that pro wrestling was riding a changing tide in society, where such content was becoming more acceptable. Conservative values of generations past started to disappear completely. A wave of animated shows came to the forefront, flushing political correctness down the drain. Primetime television started to really push the envelope.

You would think this is fine, given the late night viewing. Children would surely be tucked up in bed. Wrong. With households being able to afford more than one television, children could watch what they wanted without interruption (or supervision). Finally, with the internet exploding onto the scene, these shows could be streamed whenever (and wherever) convenient.

Your students will be watching television shows in all of their 18 rated glory. They will be exposed to controversial content on the internet from a very young age. They will be playing 18 rated video games. In other words, mentally, they will have grown up very fast, perhaps too fast. The media would want you to believe that such exposure is signalling doom and gloom. Let's look at this critically. Does the exposure to such content really impact your teaching? Does it impact their behaviour around school and in your classroom? With your expectations laid out and your rules enforced, this shouldn't really be an issue for any teacher. Just because students are exposed to more inappropriate language on television or the internet, and even if they use it frequently outside of school, there is no reason for them to use such language in your classroom.

There is no reason for their behaviour to be anything different from what you expect it to be. Well, that's how it should be. We know that doesn't always work in practice...

The value of education

My experience suggests that most parents will support you, knowing that you have the best interests of their children in mind. However, there are situations where the value of education will not truly be understood by parents.

Take a parent who was perhaps educated up to GCSE Level (or O Level). Let's assume that they did not attempt any further study. Perhaps they went out into the world of work and made a success of themselves, or perhaps they started their own business. In such a situation, it is conceivable for a parent not to fully understand the value of education or have a desire to engage with it completely. That extra push from home may not be present, especially if there is an assumption that the children will be joining the family business after their GCSEs are complete. Of course, it could go the other way. A parent's lack of engagement with education could lead to them seeing real potential in their children pursuing education to the highest level, and thus providing the support required.

Alternatively, you may deal with parents who provide a lot of lip service, but take no real action to work with you in partnership. Still, in my experience, most parents will be supportive of your efforts to educate their children. But sometimes, you do have to educate the parents as much as the students.

Growing up, I was very lucky. My parents took an active role in guiding me. They helped me make important decisions in regards to my education - e.g. what GCSEs and A Levels to pick, what university course would be right for me, what career options would be ideal, etc. They had the knowledge and experience to help me along my path in life. Without their support, I would not be writing this book today. When I entered the teaching profession, I wanted to assume that most students would have access to the same level of guidance and support at home. I soon came to realise that I had to adjust my expectations.

The exams factory

We have touched on this previously. However, it is worth mentioning again. Schools are under pressure to get good results. To get results, students are pushed to score the best possible marks on test papers. That doesn't sound too bad does it? The tests in question are the GCSE and A Level exams. Teachers feel the strain. Students feel the strain. Still doesn't sound too bad? Well let's look at this from another viewpoint. The result of this process is quite often the exercise of 'teaching to the test', and doing nothing more.

What more should teachers do, beyond teach to the test? Well hopefully, you have the ability to answer that question. I shall say no more, apart from consider the notion of teaching your subject versus teaching to the test. Also consider the idea of being able to do both successfully!

The health and safety culture

If you enter the teaching profession, you can't escape the health and safety culture. Want to run a school trip? Be prepared to be turned down depending on the level of risk involved. Wait. Your request to run the trip was approved? Be prepared to fill out an endless stream of paperwork. It is a sign of our times. This is something that you can't escape. It is endemic across the public sector. Your best bet is to work with the system, ensuring that all necessary paperwork is completed on time. Did you remember to take out insurance? Do you have a detailed understanding of student medical conditions? One could argue that the paperwork is there for good reason - i.e. to ensure all eventualities are covered and risks are mitigated. When a disaster is averted, you will be glad that you filled out that paperwork!

Technology will take over?

Let's end the chapter on a high note. Close your eyes and imagine the following. You are a student of the future. You wake up and turn on your virtual reality helmet. Forgot to charge your helmet? No problem. It has an infinite power source - some type of mineral that was mined from the moon. Your lesson is beamed down to you by an artificially intelligent being. It lives in the cloud with lots of other artificially intelligent beings that have taken over running the country, hospitals and law enforcement. Technology has taken over (by force).

Ok, we are a long way off from that. You have nothing to fear (yet). Teachers will still be employed to teach. Your major concern will eventually be a politician saying: "those VR helmets are a great idea, let's order one for every student and cut spending on actual teachers". Hopefully, we are a long way off from that too.

Conclusion

Some of the wider challenges discussed in the chapter are overstated by the media and societal hysteria. Your aim is to develop your practice, such that these challenges have a minimal impact on your teaching. Your classroom, your rules, your expectations. See what happens.

27. Twitter heaven

I maintain a reasonably active presence on Twitter. I thought it would be a good idea to collate a series of my most recent tweets. Some of the tweets are motivational in nature (usually involving cake, chocolate and other sugary treats). Some are hints and tips which summarise a few of the ideas we have looked at in the last twenty-six chapters.

30/7/14
No computers? No problem. Let's go old school. Paper for the win.

2/8/14
Certain tv shows would be great teaching resources... Suits seasons 1-3 and Breaking Bad seasons 1-5 for PSHCEE?

1/9/14
NQTs, School Direct or Teachfirst staff starting out this week: be confident, be brave. Make a difference. #Nqt #teachfirst #schooldirect

2/9/14
Day 2 of new term: Panic & stress? Ok... but remember to breathe! Step back, reflect, and move forward. #Nqt #teachfirst #schooldirect #pgce

3/9/14
Day 3 of new term - hoping panic and stress levels are reducing slightly - if not, indulge in cake! #Nqt #teachfirst #schooldirect #pgce

4/9/14
Day4 of new term-hoping everyone is organised/engaged(or at least surviving).If not-no worries.Give it time! #Nqt #teachfirst #schooldirect

5/9/14
Day5 of new term is over-what does the weekend mean to you?-gym,cake,friends,family,or tv?-or all of these? #Nqt #teachfirst #schooldirect

6/9/14

First weekend of new term. Are you relaxing, working, or doing both? #Nqt #teachfirst #schooldirect #pgce #newterm #teacher

6/9/14

Cutting back:bought £1 cookies rather than nice £1.50 cookies...yes, I can actually taste the difference. Never again. #nqt #pgce #cookies

6/9/14

How are you relaxing this weekend? My first Saturday off in months-a run, Kindle, and House of Cards S2. #pgce #nqt #schooldirect #teachfirst

6/9/14

Schools should use this to promote dangers of sugary drinks..simple...effective http://youtu.be/MqTH5Il1Stl via @YouTube #nqt #pgce #schooldirect

8/9/14

Relaxation = Treadmill in the dark, with iPod playing & reading Kindle. #selfpublish #kindle #nqt #pgce #schooldirect #author #starterguide

9/9/14

A new week. Energy levels high? Ready for what the week will bring? #Nqt #teachfirst #schooldirect #pgce

11/9/14

Weekend starts tomorrow night. Cookies? Marking? Gym? Tv? Plan ahead now. Maximise those minutes. #Nqt #teachfirst #schooldirect #pgce #Relax

12/9/14

Incline walking to start off the weekend, followed by cookies. Marvellous. How are you relaxing this weekend? #pgce #Nqt #relax #weekend

13/9/14

@tes #PGCEtips Technology used for the sake of using it is pointless - it requires a purpose and planned thought.

13/9/14
@tes #PGCEtips Look carefully at your whiteboard/IWB.Can all students read what is presented?Place yourself at the back of the class & check

13/9/14
@tes #PGCEtips Your PGCE takes up a lot of time/energy-a positive obsession.Counter this by finding another obsession/hobby- e.g. a good book

13/9/14
@tes #PGCEtips Look after your favourite pen. Never lend it out. Look after it. See if you can go a whole term without losing it!

13/9/14
@tes #PGCEtips Create a mental separation between work stress and home life. Easier said than done - but can be achieved in time.

13/9/14
@tes #PGCEtips Develop an organised system of marking and planning early on - e.g. Tues night Y7 marking, Wed night Y10 planning, etc.

13/9/14
@tes #PGCEtips Don't be goaded into confrontation in the classroom - calm, civil, yet firm - in control. Choose your language carefully.

13/9/14
@tes #PGCEtips Don't be afraid of making mistakes. Learn from them and move on: Learn from the past. Evaluate the present. Shape the future.

13/9/14
@tes #PGCEtips Plan out relaxation in advance - e.g. 3 hour marathon of fav tv series on Sat night. Gives you something to look forward to.

13/9/14
@tes #PGCEtips Find a quiet place in school (& home) that you can work without being bothered/interrupted. Productivity increases!

14/9/14

@tes #PGCEtips Get involved in whole-school activities, e.g. football club, drama club, etc. Increases your whole-school presence/visibility.

14/9/14

@tes #PGCEtips Before going on PGCE placement 1, work out other transport routes / ways in - never know when your usual route will fail you!

14/9/14

@tes #PGCEtips Before you start your day - check the equipment is working (your classroom PC, projector, etc). Know who to call if needed!

14/9/14

@tes #PGCEtips Always be on time to your lessons - setting a good example for your students, who you are a role model for.

14/9/14

@tes #PGCEtips When starting in your placement school, get a copy of the school map and explore before you start teaching.

14/9/14

@tes #PGCEtips Electronic & paper mediums for your task lists- both have pros and cons. Using a mixture of both may yield positive results.

14/9/14

@tes #PGCEtips Be brave, this will be unlike anything you have ever done before. A chance to make a real and tangible positive difference.

15/9/14

Good luck those starting #PGCE training today at university. Be brave. Life-changing opportunity. #traineeteacher #studenteacher #PGCEtips

15/9/14

Look after your old certificates! #pgce #nqt #schooldirect #traineeteacher The Simpsons - I Am So Smart: http://youtu.be/DhrfhjLd9e4 via @YouTube

16/9/14

Started your #PGCE yesterday & feeling overwhelmed with information overload? To be expected. Solution? Organised notes, task lists & sleep!

16/9/14

Trying to get your head round your #PGCE course? Remember what a special opportunity you have. Tweet #NQT teachers & see what you can learn.

16/9/14

Teaching unions can learn from Lisa Simpson? "Lisa cantando Union strike folk song:" http://youtu.be/uH_8521bePM via @YouTube #pgce #nqt #NUT

17/9/14

What behaviour mgt techniques would you apply for Homer? #pgce #pgcetips #nqt #traineeteacher #nqtchat http://youtu.be/olr9lKSa34k via @YouTube

18/9/14

Try to make what you teach relevant to the lives of the students. Will make delivery easier if they see why it matters. #pgce #pgcetips #nqt

18/9/14

Class context sheets are very useful - providing an observer with key info re: particular groups in the class #pgce #pgcetips #nqt #nqtchat

19/9/14

Consider morning routine before school/uni: Meditation? Read 30 mins of a good book? Press-ups? Something to relax you. #pgce #pgcetips #nqt

20/9/14

Using public transport can be a blessing. Time for: relaxation, reading, sleeping, thinking [unless there are delays!!] #pgcetips #pgce #nqt

20/9/14

Major congrats to those that have got through weeks 1 and/or 2 of their PGCE. Long road ahead, but very much worth it. #pgcetips #pgce #nqt

20/9/14
If only I could incorporate #Hearthstone cards into my teaching. Teaches strategic thinking/problem solving http://peachya.com/file/2014/08/hearthstone-cards.jpg ... #pgce #nqt

21/9/14
A lazy Sunday afternoon with tv and cake - or - an intense work filled Sunday getting ready for tomorrow? #PGCE #PGCEtips #NQT #schooldirect

21/9/14
"How's education supposed to make me feel smarter"-what advice would you give to Homer? http://youtu.be/8dbDJzDV1CM @YouTube #pgce #nqt #pgcetips

22/9/14
PGCE survival equation = hard work and organisation is the key = task lists and efficient scheduling wins the day. #pgce #pgcetips #nqt

25/9/14
PGCE survival equation 2 = Try to stay calm = gives you time to think before acting = manages your stress levels. #pgce #pgcetips #nqt

27/9/14
PGCE survival equation 3 = Saturday night = relax = recharge = exercise + takeaway + television + escape in a good book #pgce #pgcetips #nqt

30/9/14
Stressful day at school? - Hail To The Busdriver: http://youtu.be/zlej7l0Lmpk via @YouTube #pgce #pgcetips #nqt

1/10/14
Exercise on a Wednesday night - motivated by Homer - What's A Gym: http://youtu.be/R4i8SpNgzA4 via @YouTube #pgce #nqt

3/10/14
When observing lessons, talk to the students-will feel like you know them better - so when teaching, your confidence increases.
Start perhaps by taking parts of a lesson - rather than the full lesson.

(advice given to a beginner teacher, considering how to gain the confidence needed, when stepping up from being a classroom observer to being a classroom teacher)

28. A summary

We have covered a lot of ground in this book. For those of you that are visual learners, consider this diagram below. It is a nice summary of our journey together.

You can see a clear version here: http://goo.gl/grfz3I

29. The end

And so this is the end. Some questions to ask yourself. If you are considering entry into the profession, has this book scared you off or encouraged you to join? If you are undertaking a PGCE course, do you feel better equipped to make the most of your teaching placements and make the jump to your NQT year? If you are currently an NQT or working under the Teach First and School Direct schemes, do you feel more confident in approaching the year ahead and making informed decisions over options for further progression and promotion?

Please do note that the views in this book are my own. My slant on the teaching profession and what it has to offer. My opinion on what is expected and the standards we should uphold. Being a teacher is truly honourable. A selfless role, allowing you to shape the future of a nation. Think about that for a second (or a minute).

How will you use this power you hold? How will you be remembered? Will you be that teacher that stands out in some way, remembered by students and colleagues for a particular positive quality? The teacher that goes the extra mile when needed? The teacher that is supportive of their colleagues in times of need? The teacher that truly uses technology effectively in aiding teaching and learning? The teacher that is incredibly well organised? The teacher renowned for their incredible planning skills? The teacher that works incredibly hard, maintaining the highest standards in all respects, yet manages to master the work-life balance? Who are you really?

Writing this book was an interesting journey for me. It has helped to further shape me as a teacher. I have learned a lot from this process. We never stop learning. We never stop changing. We never stop reflecting.

I will repeat what I said at the start. If anything in this book can help you succeed and become a better practitioner, then I will truly be honoured. Mission accomplished. Thank you for reading.

Oh and one final thing. There will come a point where you will need to forget everything you have read in this book. A point where you will need to forget what others have told you and discard your own learned behaviour in the classroom. At this point, the profession will have changed. Therefore, expectations will have changed. Policy will have changed. The system will have changed. Teaching methods will have changed. Subjects taught will have changed. Whether this is the result of societal change, economic change, governmental change or cultural change, you will need to adapt. To adapt is to survive. Teaching in 1984 is different to teaching in 2014. Techniques used today are different to techniques used a generation ago. Teachers who do not adapt do not survive, or certainly struggle to operate on a daily basis. Come 2044, what kind of teacher will you be?

Learn to be your own teacher. Shape your own destiny. Whatever happens, whatever changes, don't forget why you became a teacher. Stay true to your ideals and your values.

Finally, remember that we have always had teachers from the beginning of mankind in one guise or another. There will always be a need for teachers, as long as mankind continues to thrive and/or survive. You will always be in demand for your skills and abilities (either in the teaching profession or outside of it). A lot of faith and trust is placed in you. You hold a position of responsibility that directly impacts the daily lives and future prospects of young people. Move forward with confidence, knowing that what you do on a daily basis is truly special and unique.

30. Coming soon to a Kindle near you...

Chapter three on organisation is truly a critical chapter. Even if you find yourself struggling with other areas, if you can master the art of being organised, there is certainly hope for the future.

I would even argue that you can be masterful of other areas, but an inability to be organised leads nowhere. You can be the most brilliant teacher, amazing at articulating key concepts, and classified as a 'legend' by the students. Yes, that is a good thing. It doesn't mean you are 'old'. It means you are revered and respected. However, if you forget to turn up to meetings on time, produce reports that are filled with errors, or don't know who your students are, then it is all for nothing. If you send the wrong e-mails to the wrong staff, or use your time poorly during free periods, then all of that great teaching will only take you so far. If you don't have your resources prepared for the right lessons, or can't juggle the range of different deadlines surrounding marking, assessment and whole-school events, then things will really start to fall apart.

On that basis, I have started work on a second book, based purely around the notion of being organised. Based on numerous conversations with colleagues over the years, this is an area that probably needs significant attention in the world of educational literature, yet gets brushed under the carpet in favour of other areas such as pedagogy and behaviour management.

The working title is: *Teaching in UK Secondary Schools - a PGCE, School Direct and NQT Checklist, Being Organised from September through till Christmas*. The book proposes a checklist of items to consider for the following time periods: before the start of the September term, the first three weeks of teaching, post October half-term, and then Christmas and beyond.

I am hoping to make this second book available through both electronic and physical mediums.

Further details will appear on my website (http://www.techlearn.org.uk) or through my Twitter account (@TechLearnUK).

Printed in Great Britain
by Amazon.co.uk, Ltd.,
Marston Gate.